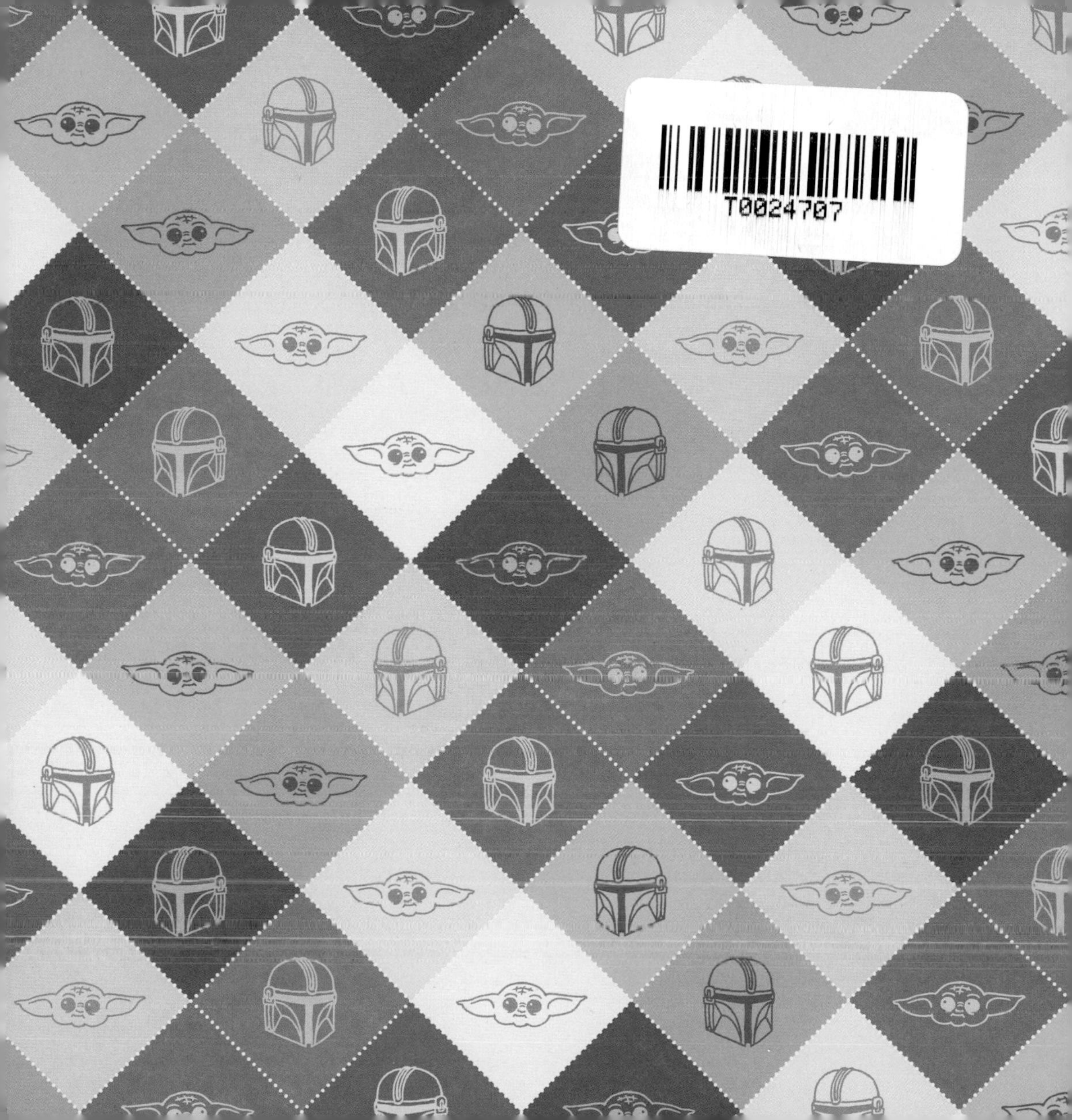

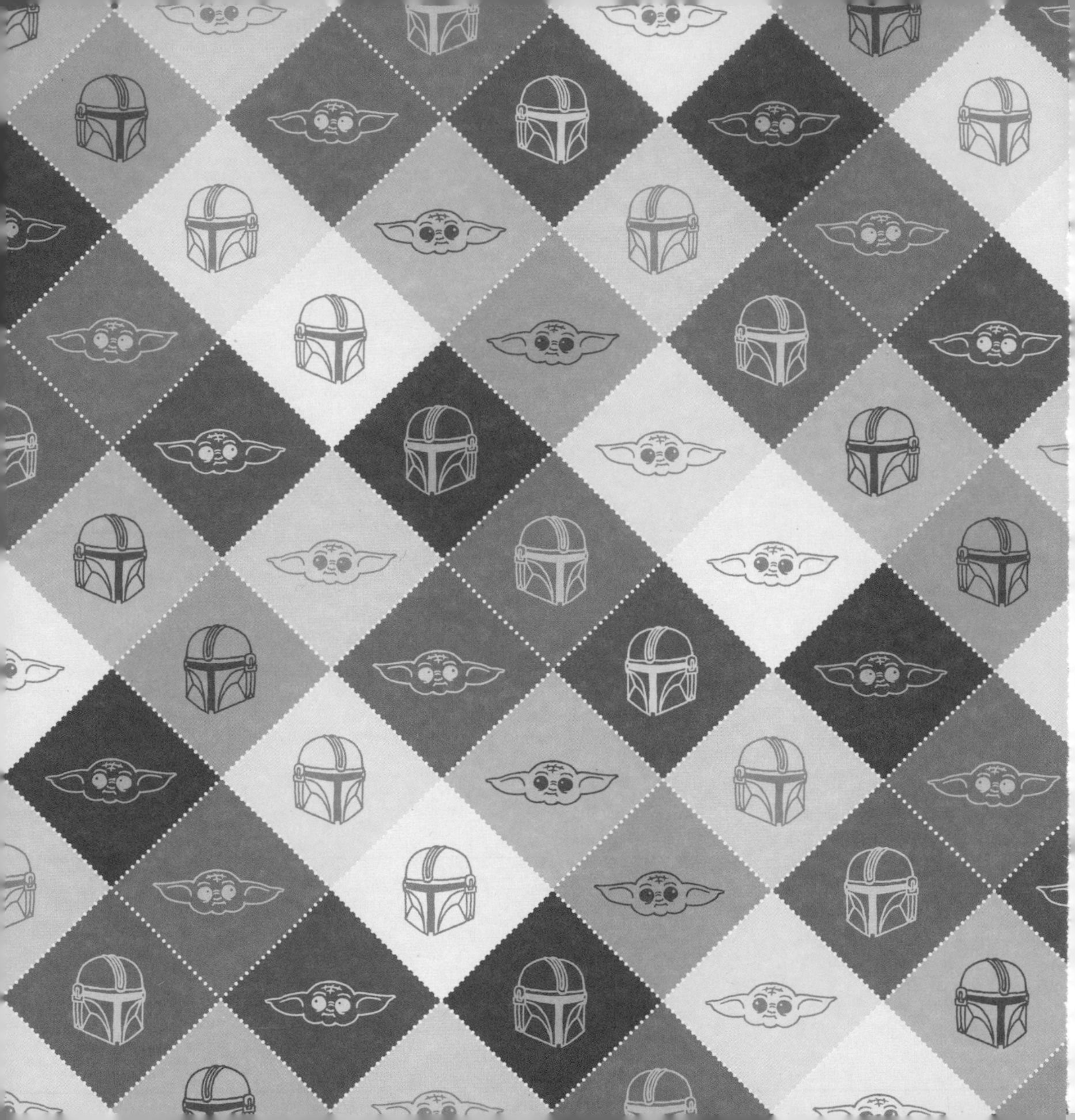

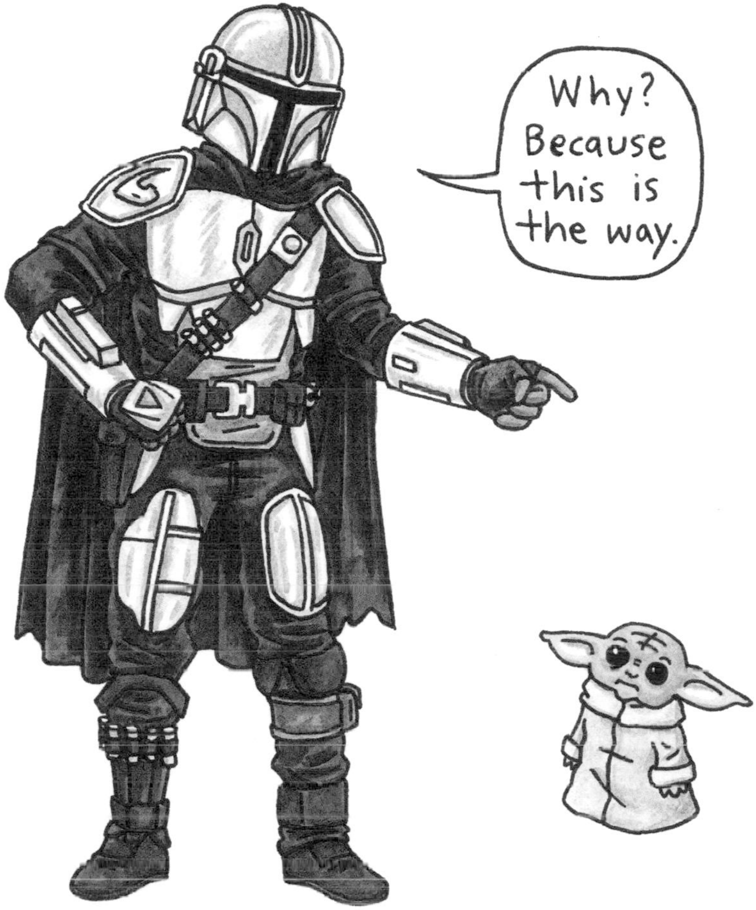
Why? Because this is the way.

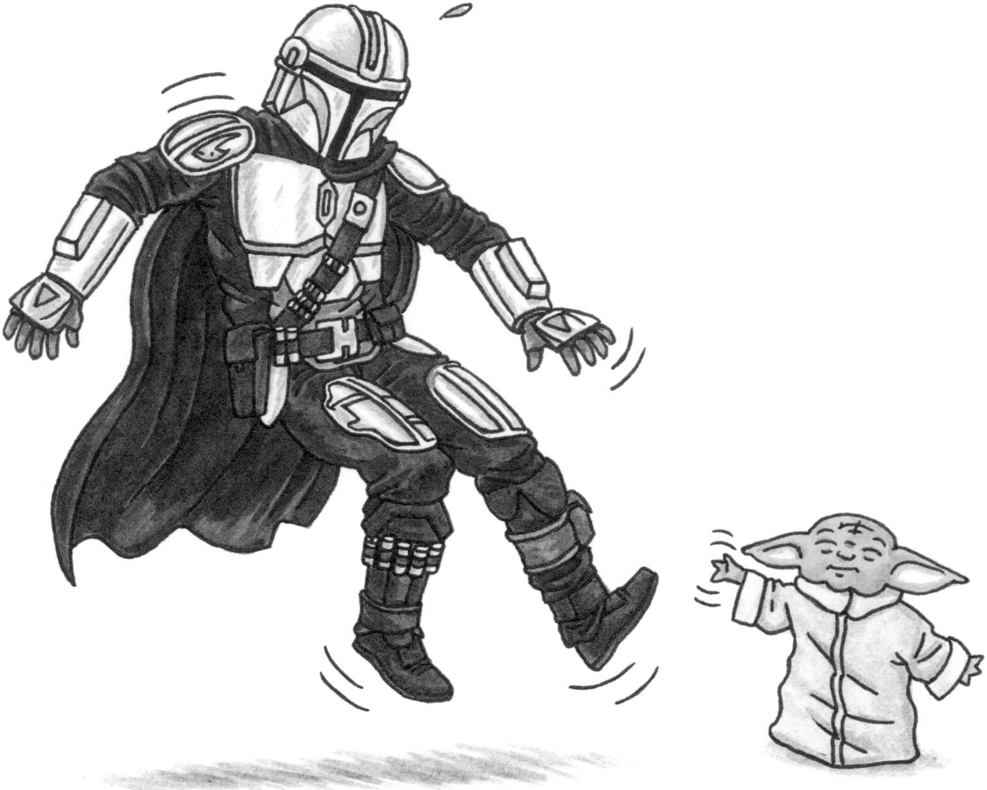

THE MANDALORIAN
and Child

BY
JEFFREY
BROWN

CHRONICLE BOOKS
SAN FRANCISCO

LIBRARY OF CONGRESS CATALOGING-IN-PUBLICATION DATA IS AVAILABLE.

ISBN 978-1-7972-2369-8

MANUFACTURED IN CANADA.

MIX
Paper from responsible sources
FSC www.fsc.org FSC® C103567

WRITTEN AND DRAWN BY JEFFREY BROWN.
DESIGNED BY NEIL EGAN AND LIAM FLANAGAN.

THANKS TO STEVE MOCKUS, J.W. RINZLER, MARC GERALD, MY FAMILY, AND ALL OF MY READERS. SPECIAL THANKS TO RYAN GERMICK AND MICHEAL LOPEZ AT GOOGLE FOR THE ORIGINAL INSPIRATION TO MAKE *DARTH VADER AND SON.*

10 9 8 7 6 5 4 3 2 1

CHRONICLE BOOKS LLC
680 SECOND STREET
SAN FRANCISCO, CALIFORNIA 94107

WWW.CHRONICLEBOOKS.COM

WWW.STARWARS.COM

A long time ago
in a galaxy far, far away....

MANDALORIAN BOUNTY HUNTER
DIN DJARIN HAS TRAVELED
THROUGHOUT THE OUTER RIM
BATTLING IMPERIALS AND CATCHING
NEFARIOUS CRIMINALS. NOW, HE MUST
FACE HIS TOUGHEST CHALLENGE YET:
TAKING CARE OF...

...THE CHILD.

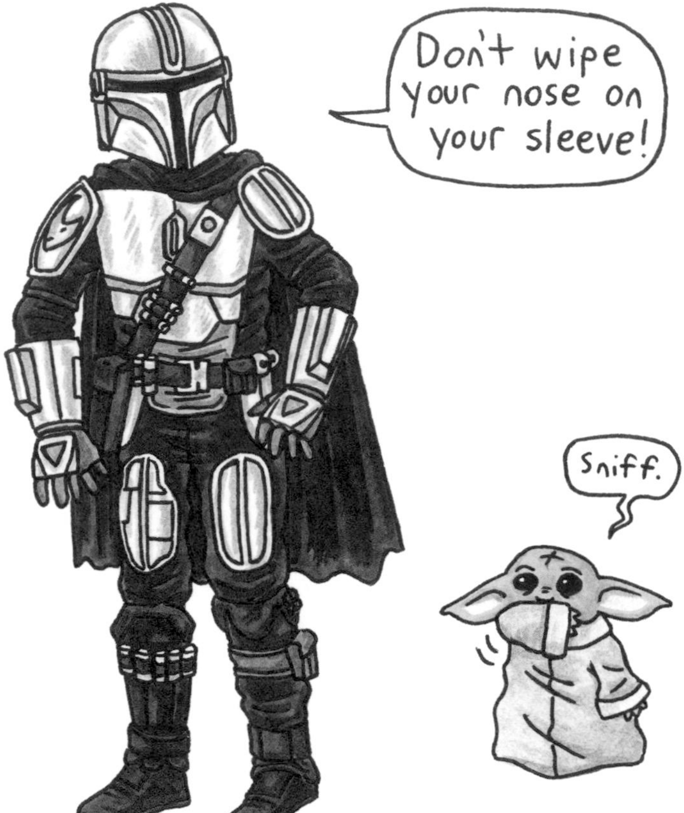
Don't wipe your nose on your sleeve!
Sniff.

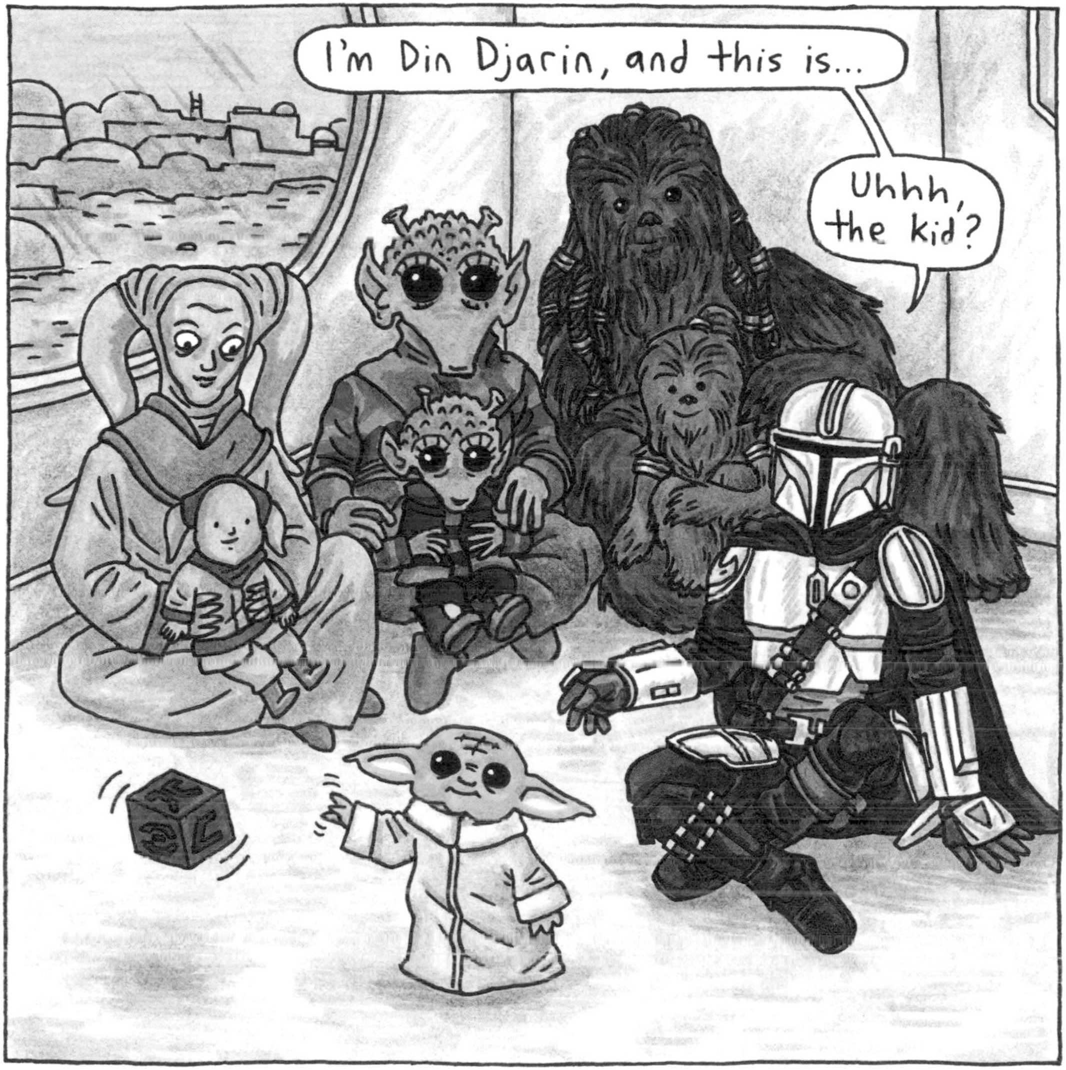
I'm Din Djarin, and this is...
Uhhh, the kid?

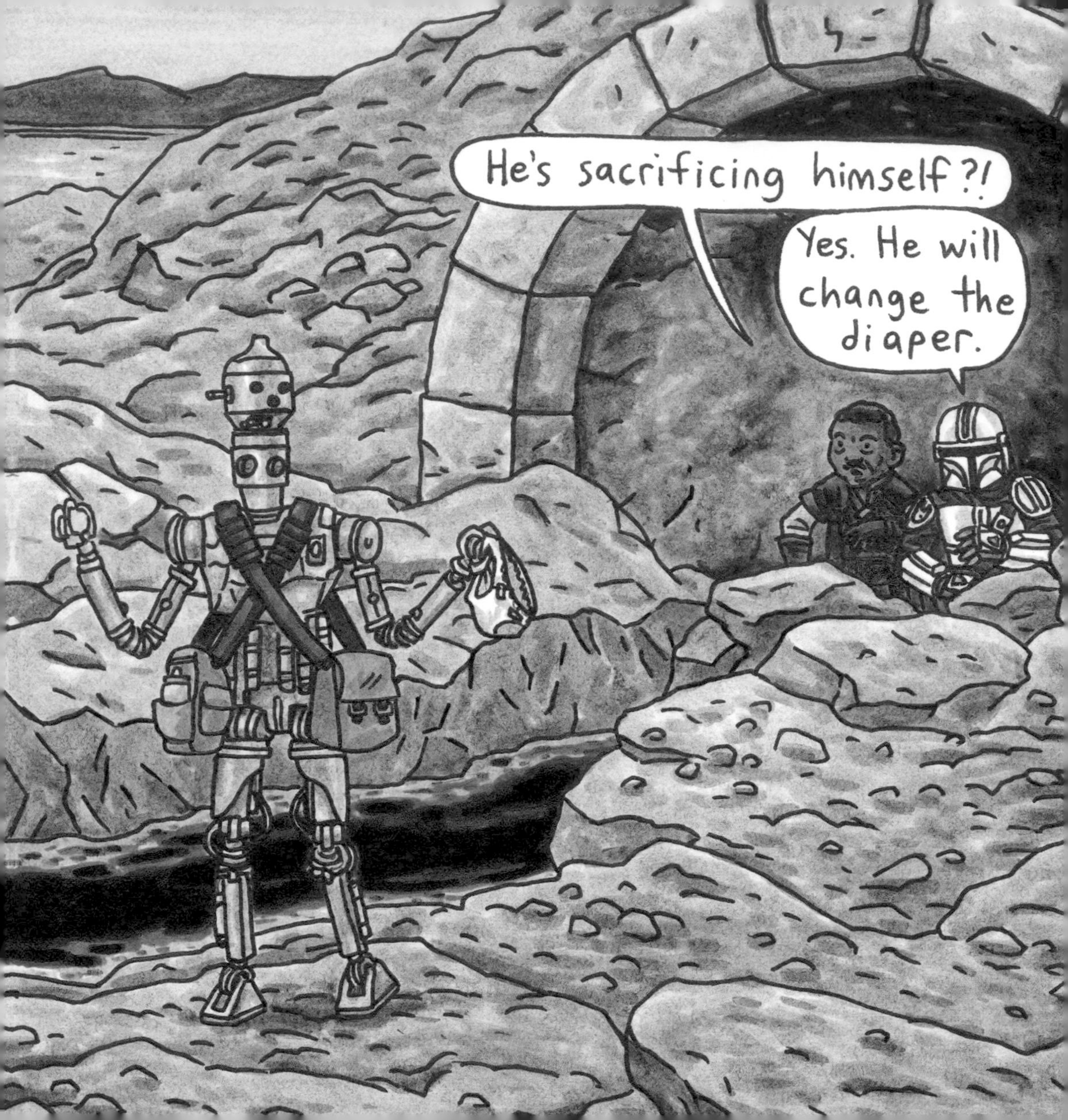
He's sacrificing himself?!
Yes. He will change the diaper.

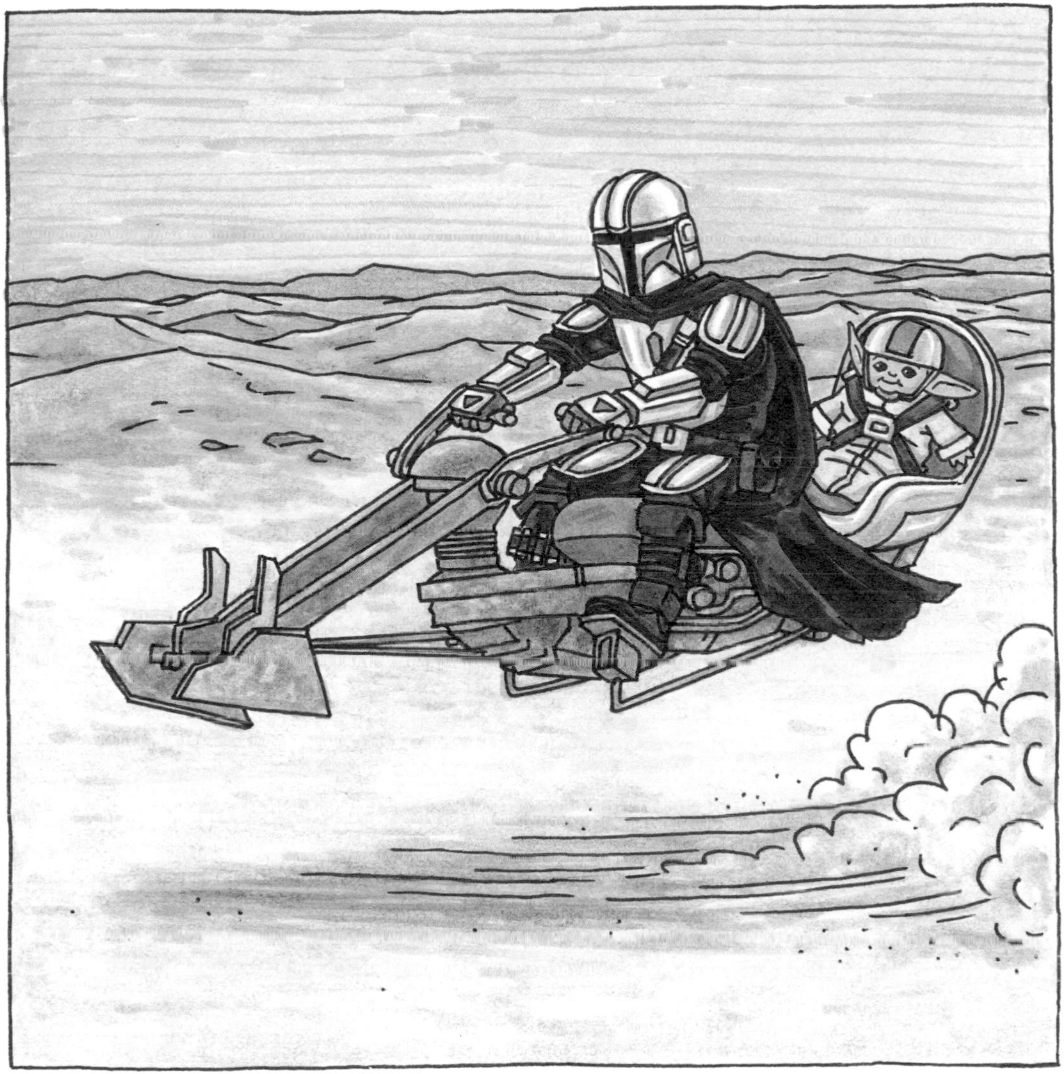

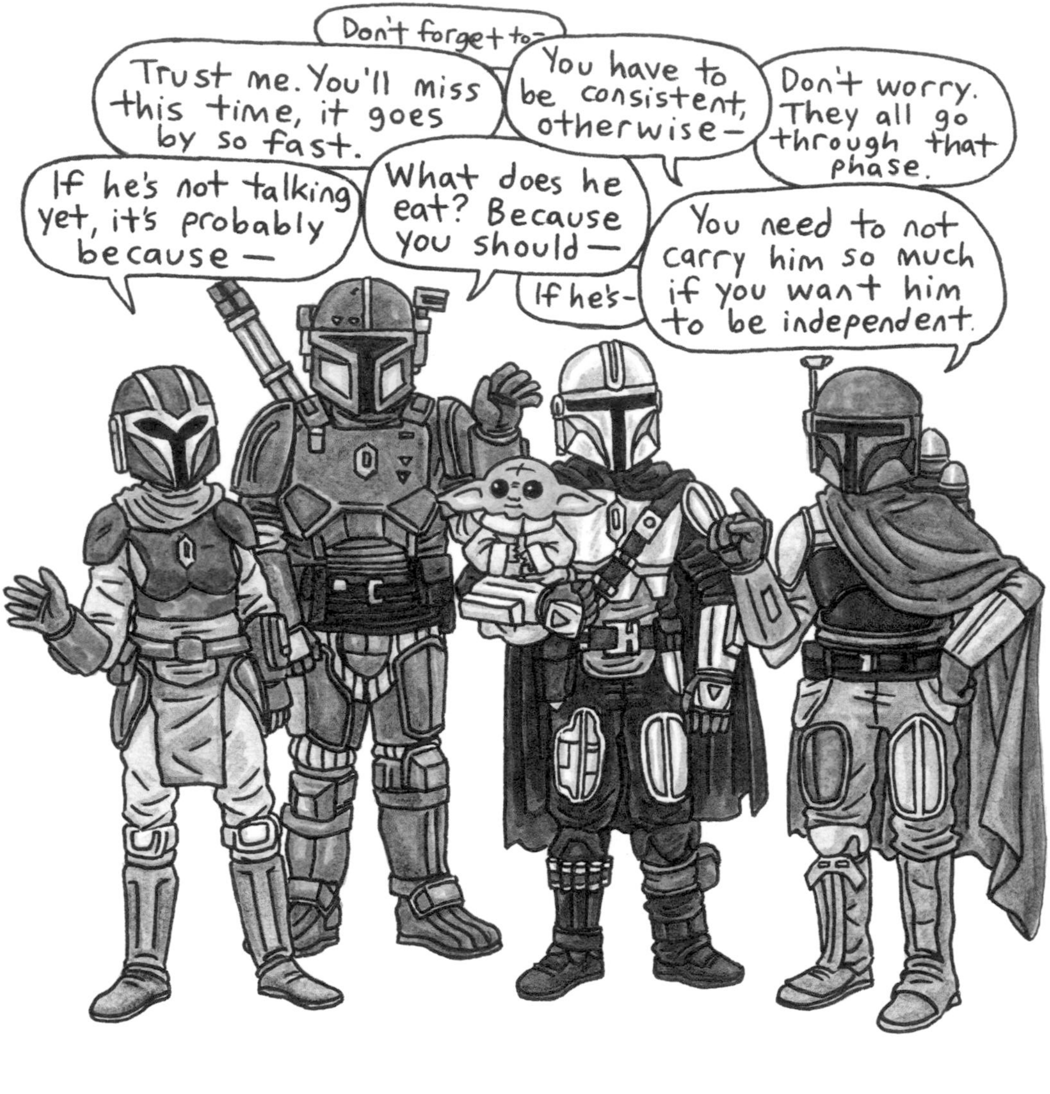
Don't forget to-
Trust me. You'll miss this time, it goes by so fast.
You have to be consistent, otherwise—
Don't worry. They all go through that phase.
If he's not talking yet, it's probably because—
What does he eat? Because you should—
If he's-
You need to not carry him so much if you want him to be independent.

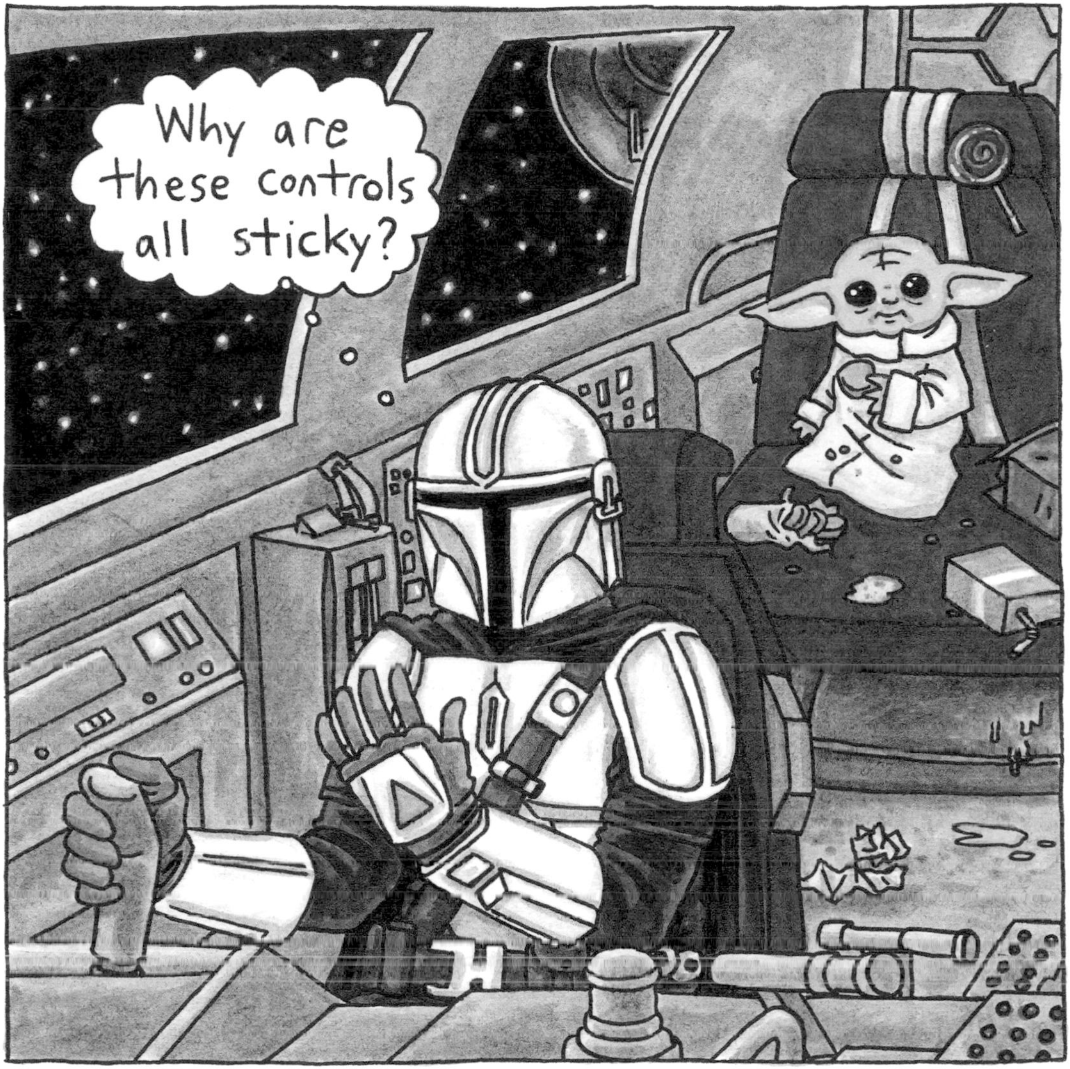
Why are these controls all sticky?

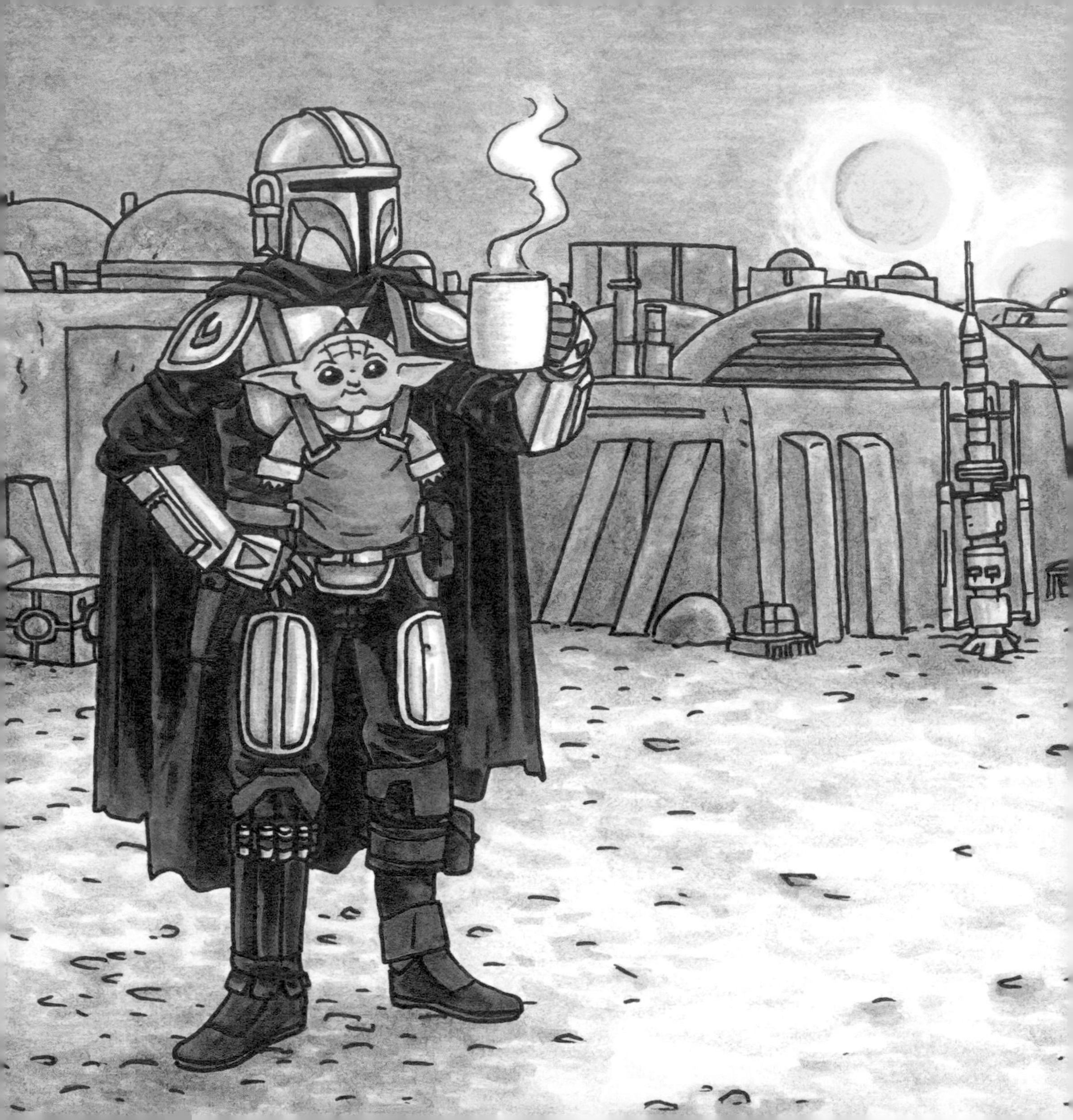

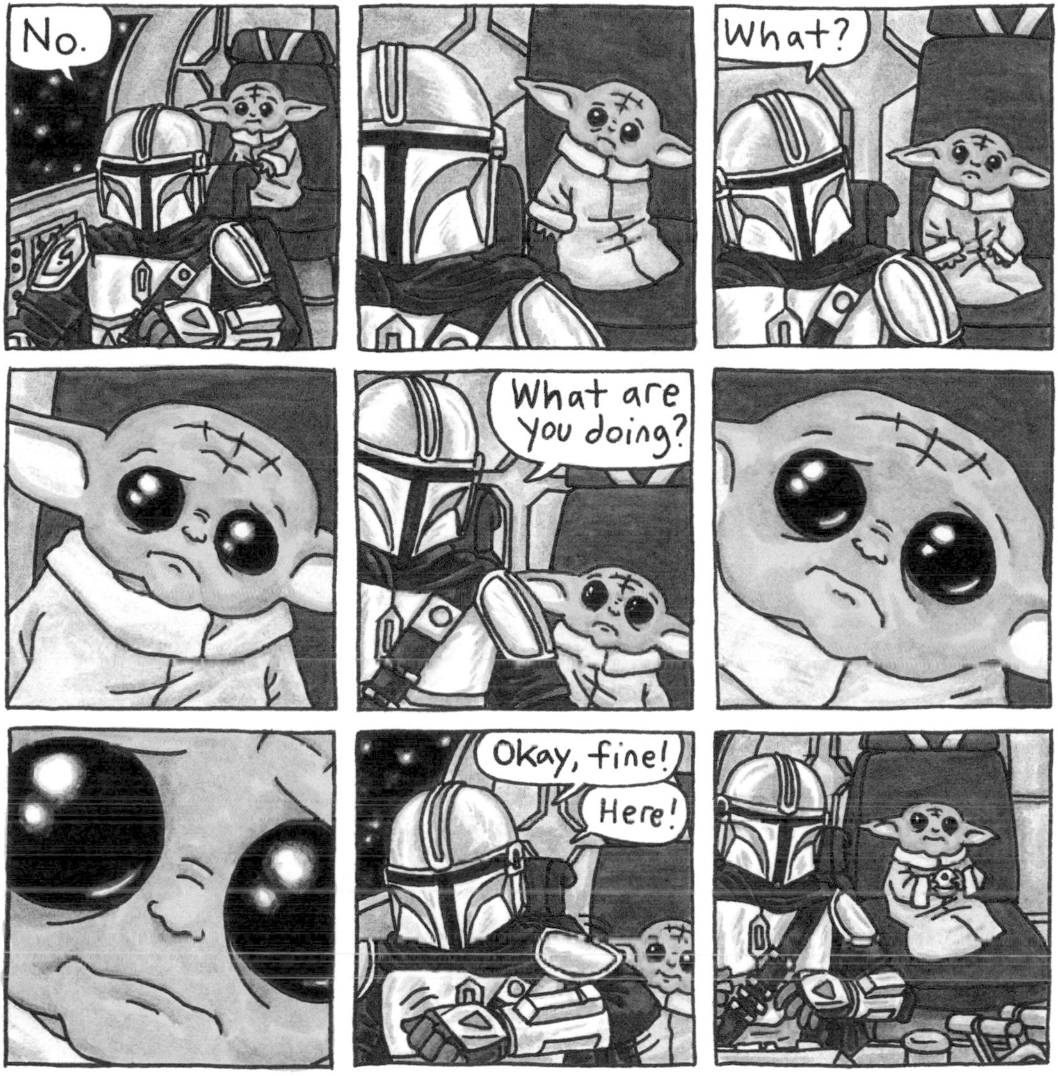
No.
What?
What are you doing?
Okay, fine!
Here!

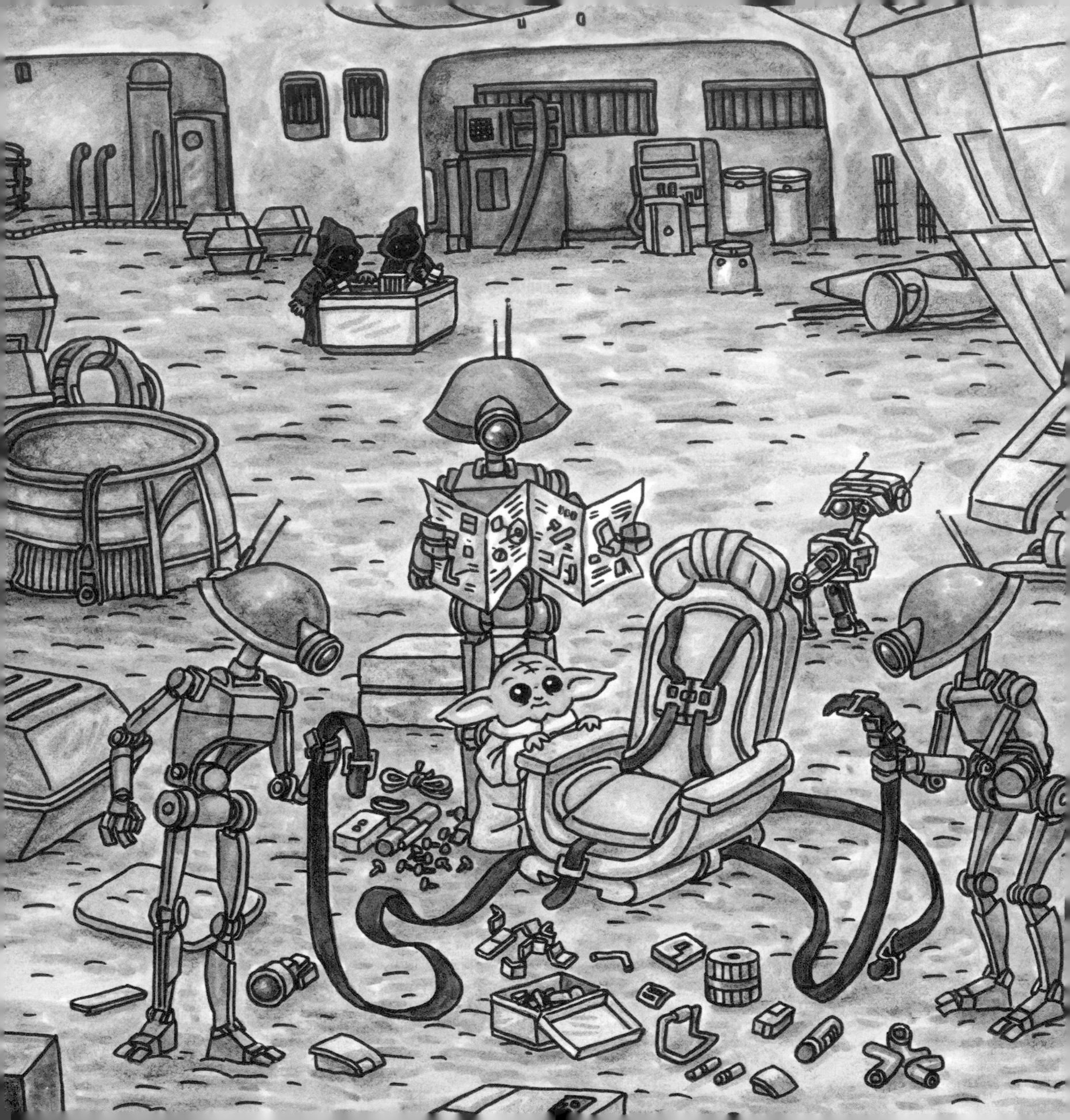

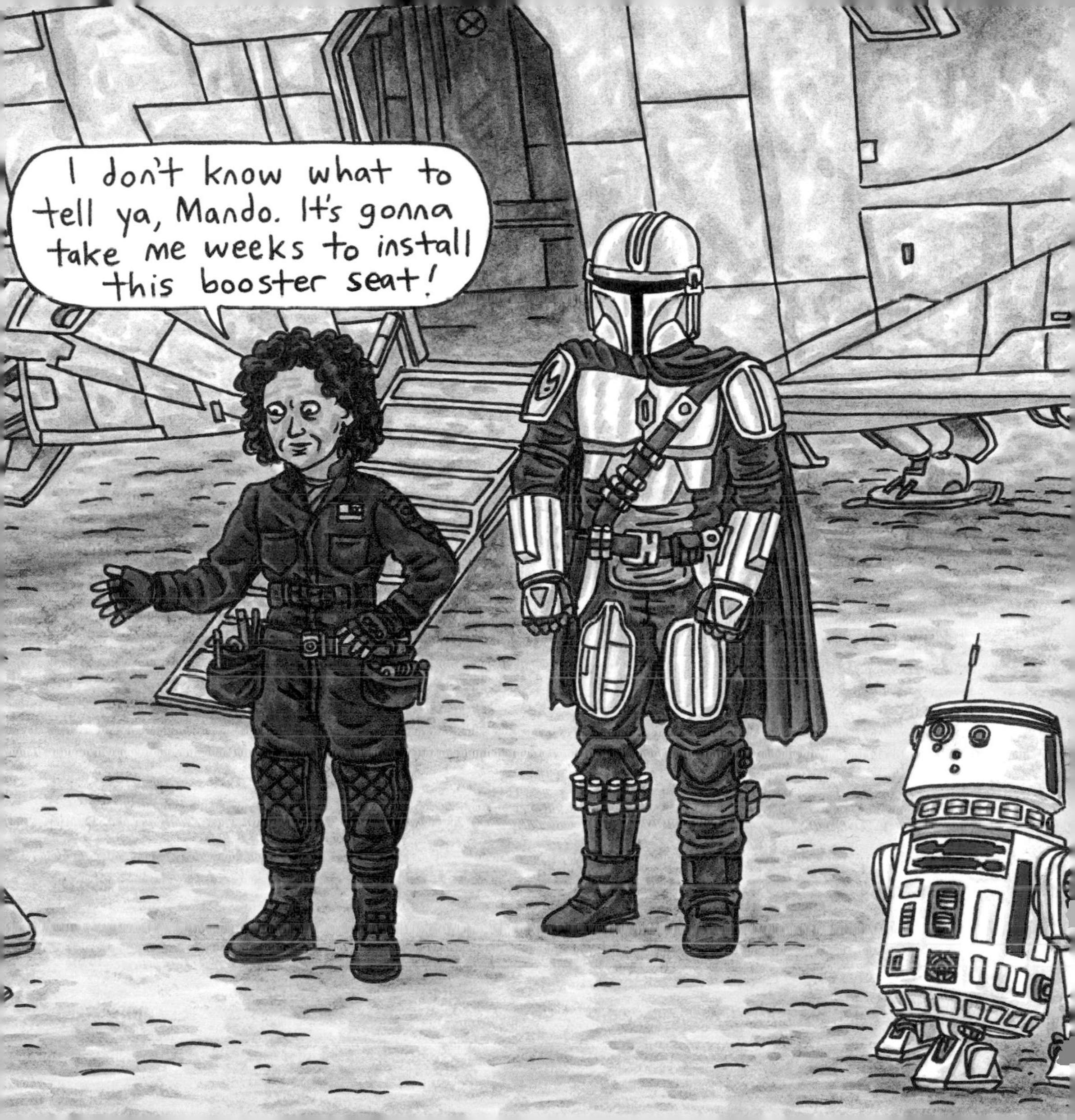
I don't know what to tell ya, Mando. It's gonna take me weeks to install this booster seat!

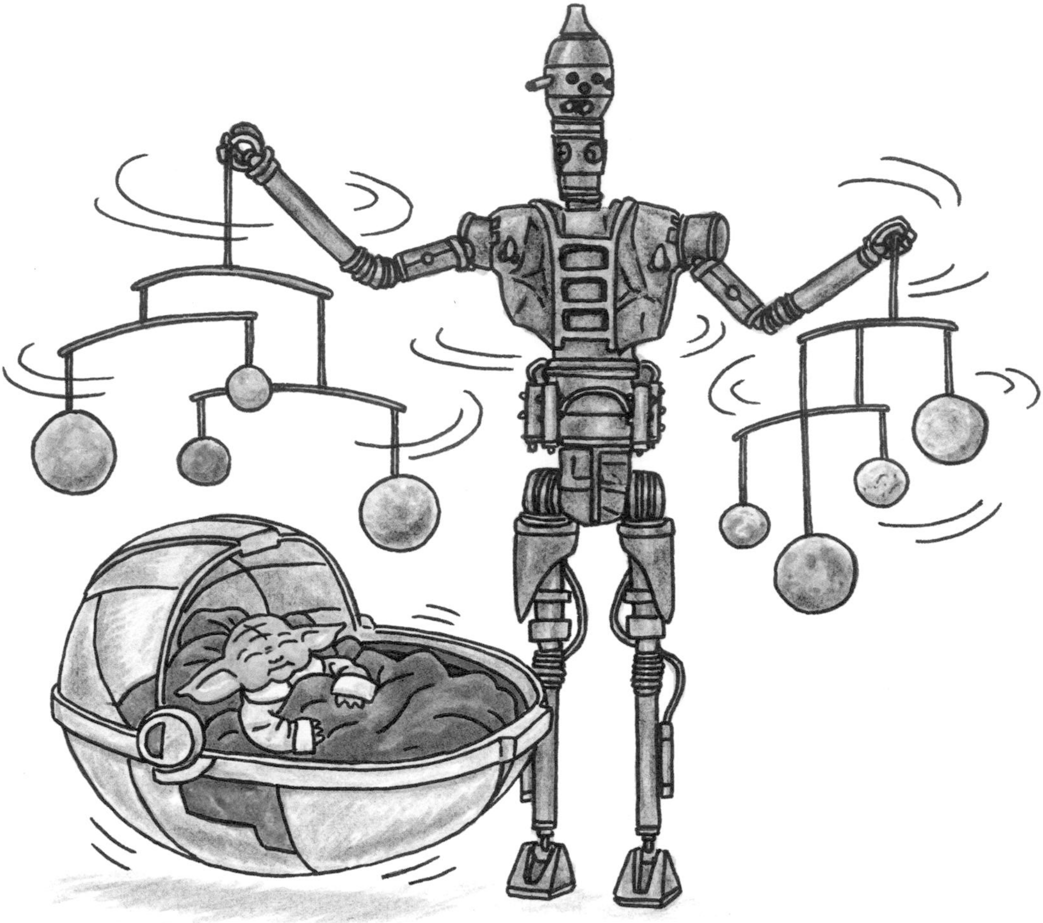

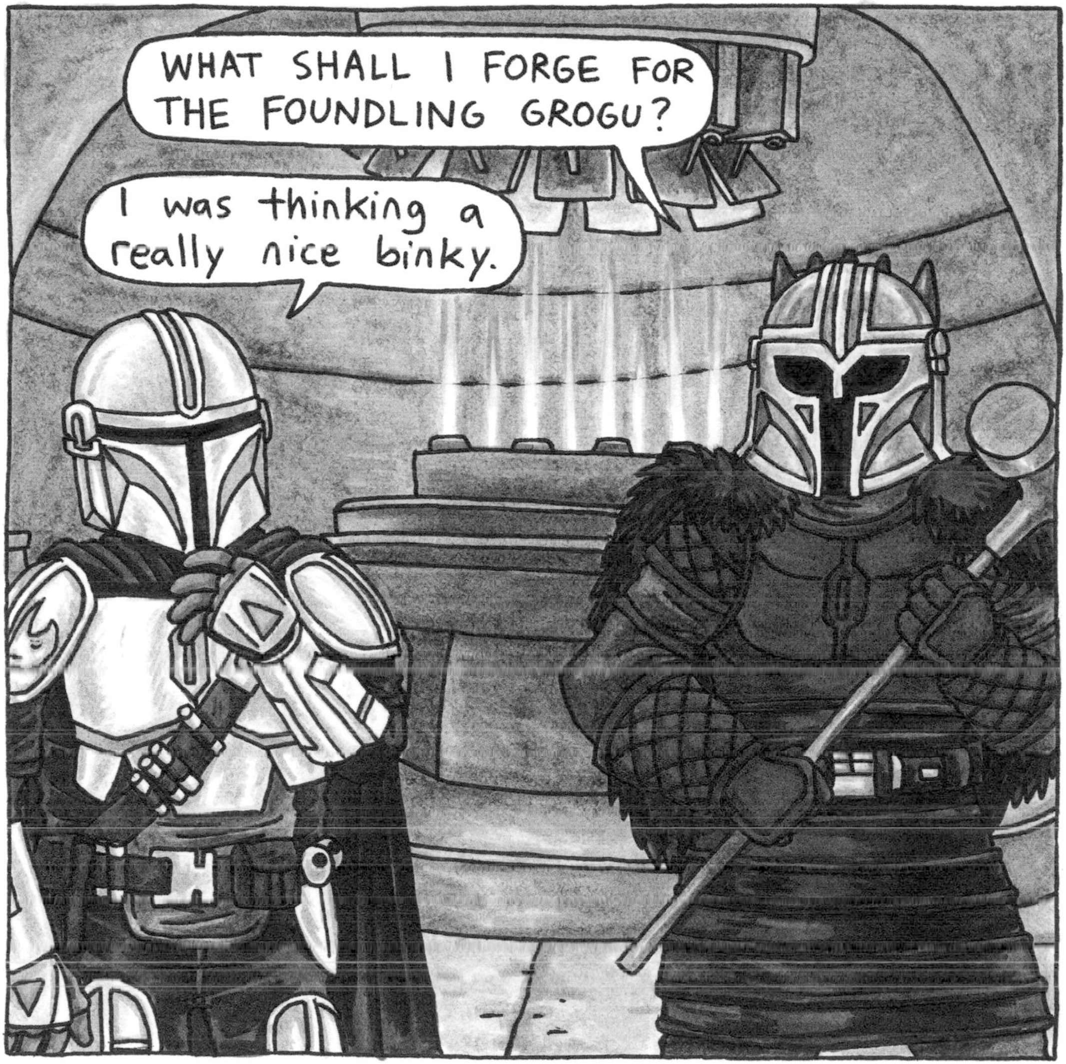
WHAT SHALL I FORGE FOR THE FOUNDLING GROGU?
I was thinking a really nice binky.

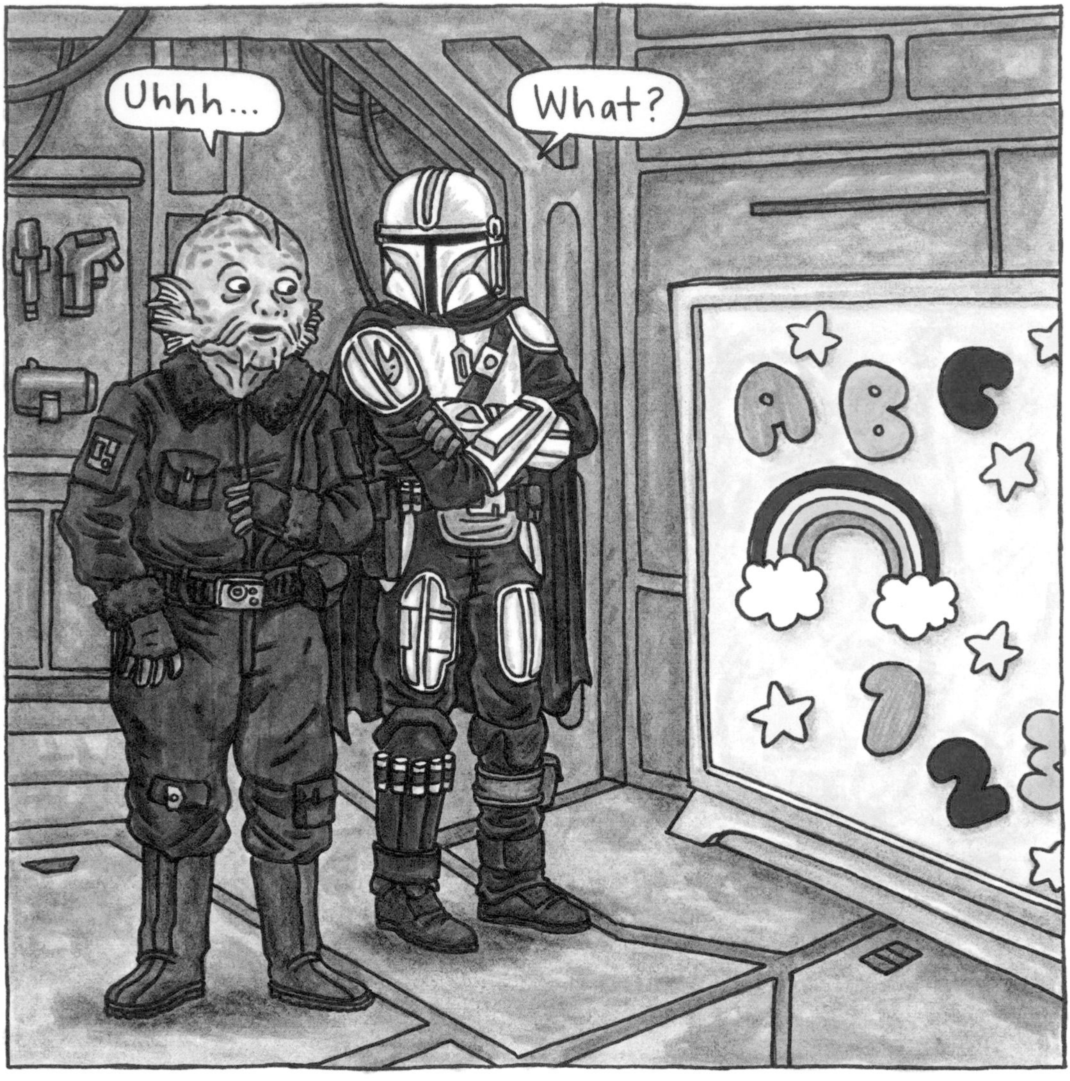
Uhhh...
What?
ABC
123

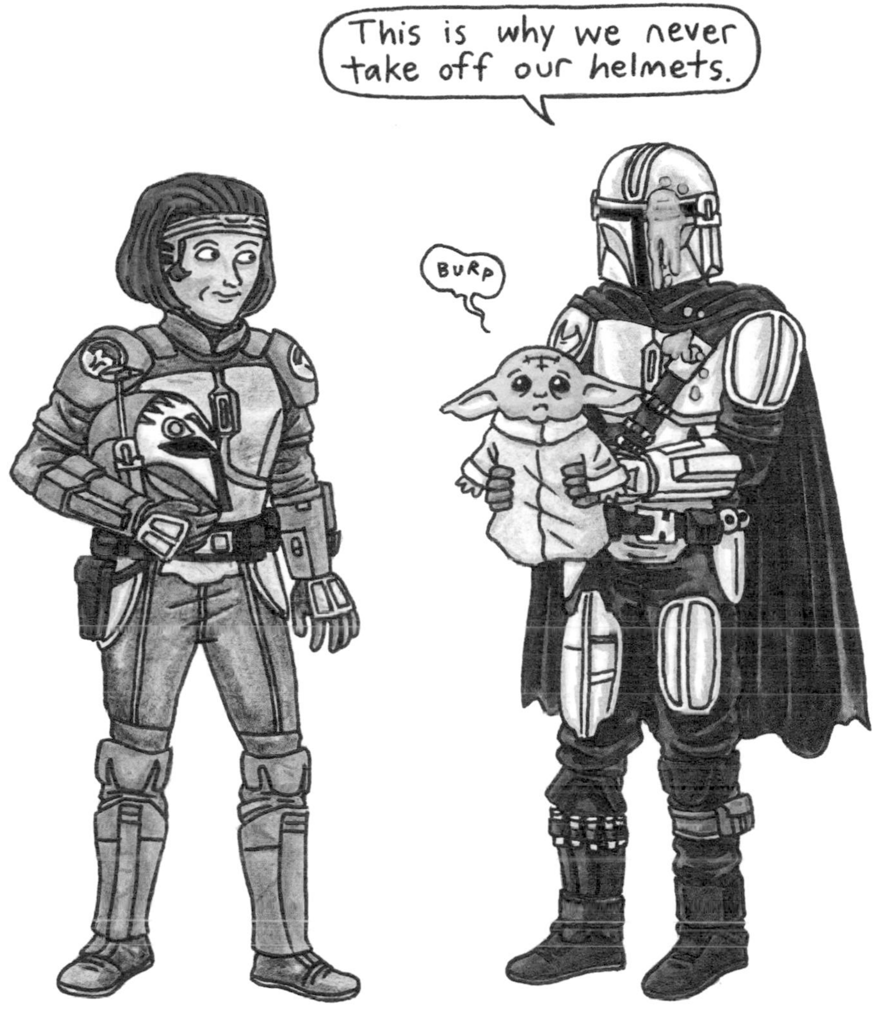
This is why we never take off our helmets.
BURP

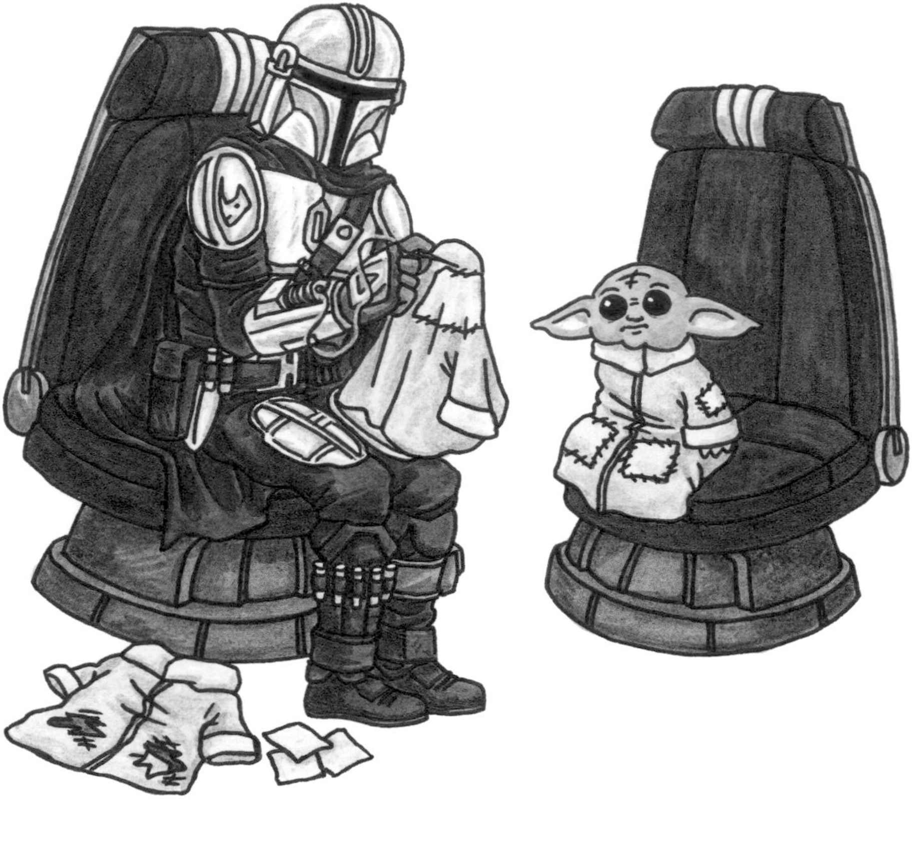

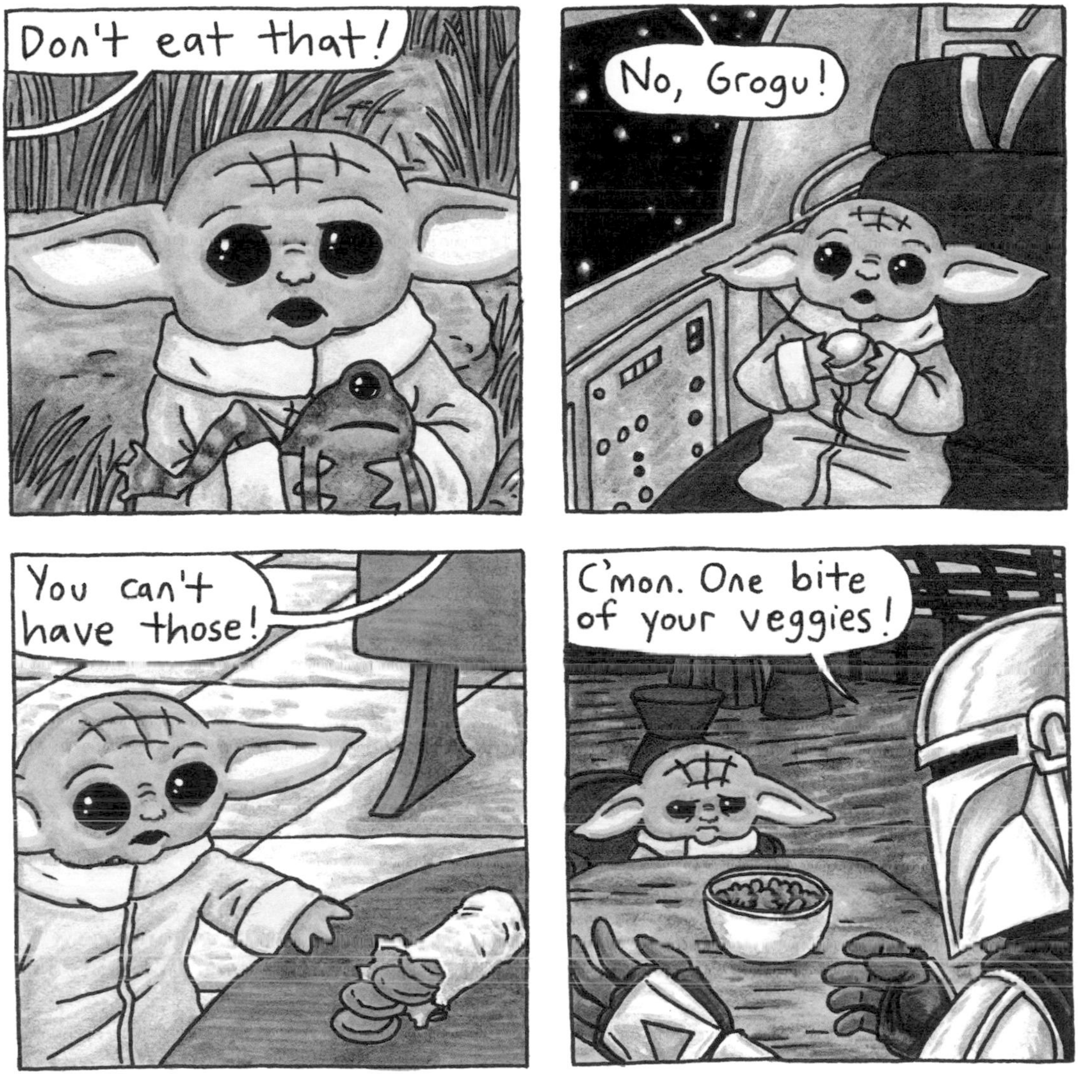
Don't eat that!
No, Grogu!
You can't have those!
C'mon. One bite of your veggies!

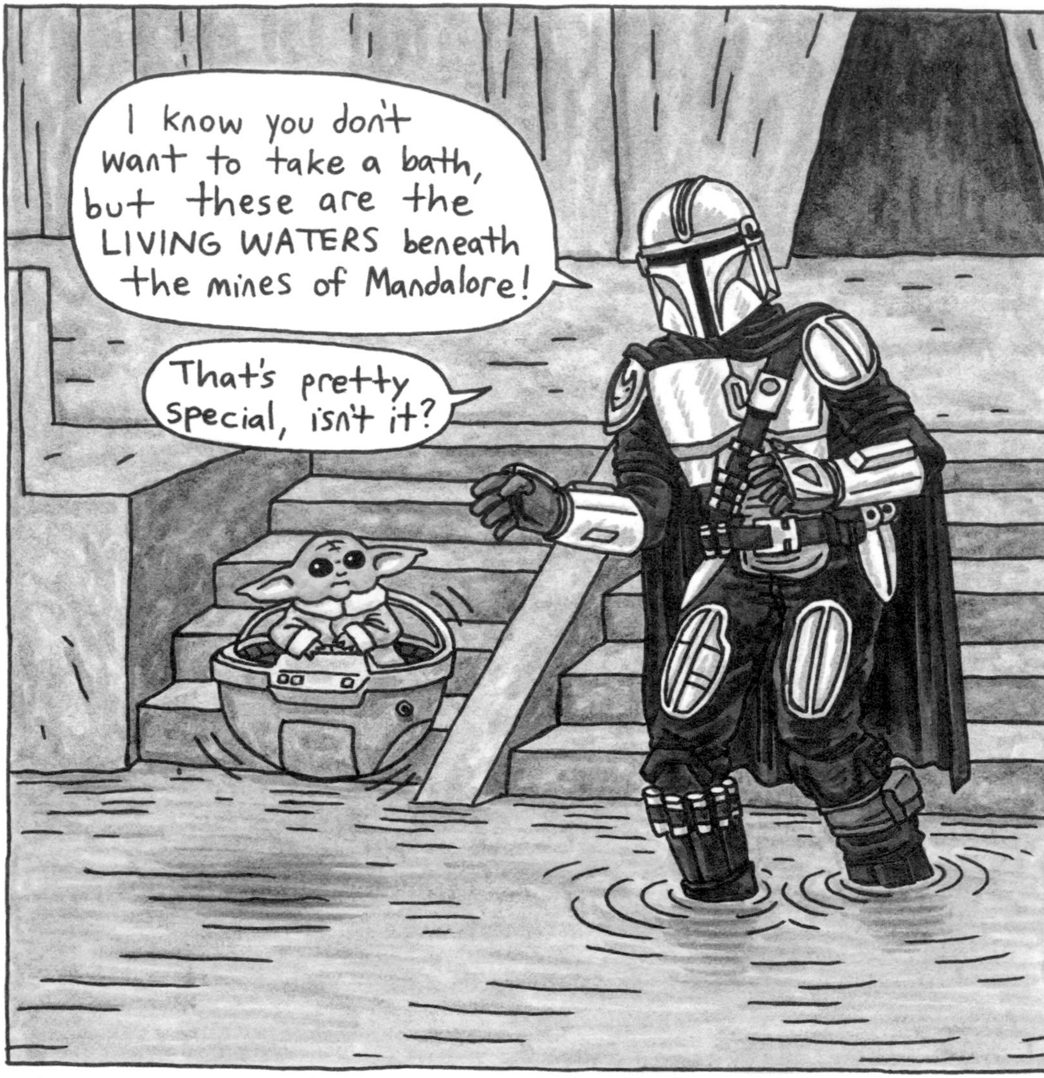
I know you don't want to take a bath, but these are the LIVING WATERS beneath the mines of Mandalore!
That's pretty special, isn't it?

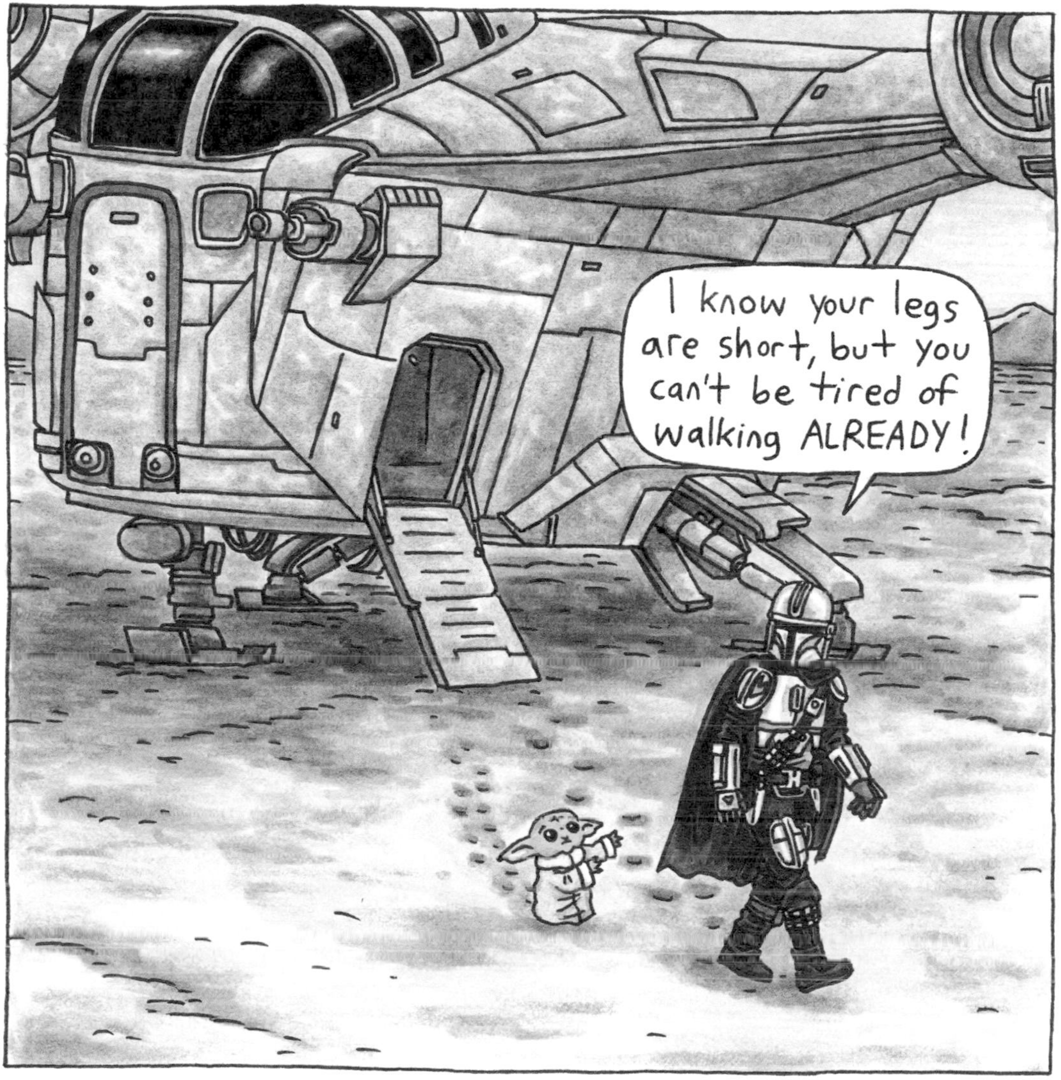
I know your legs are short, but you can't be tired of walking ALREADY!

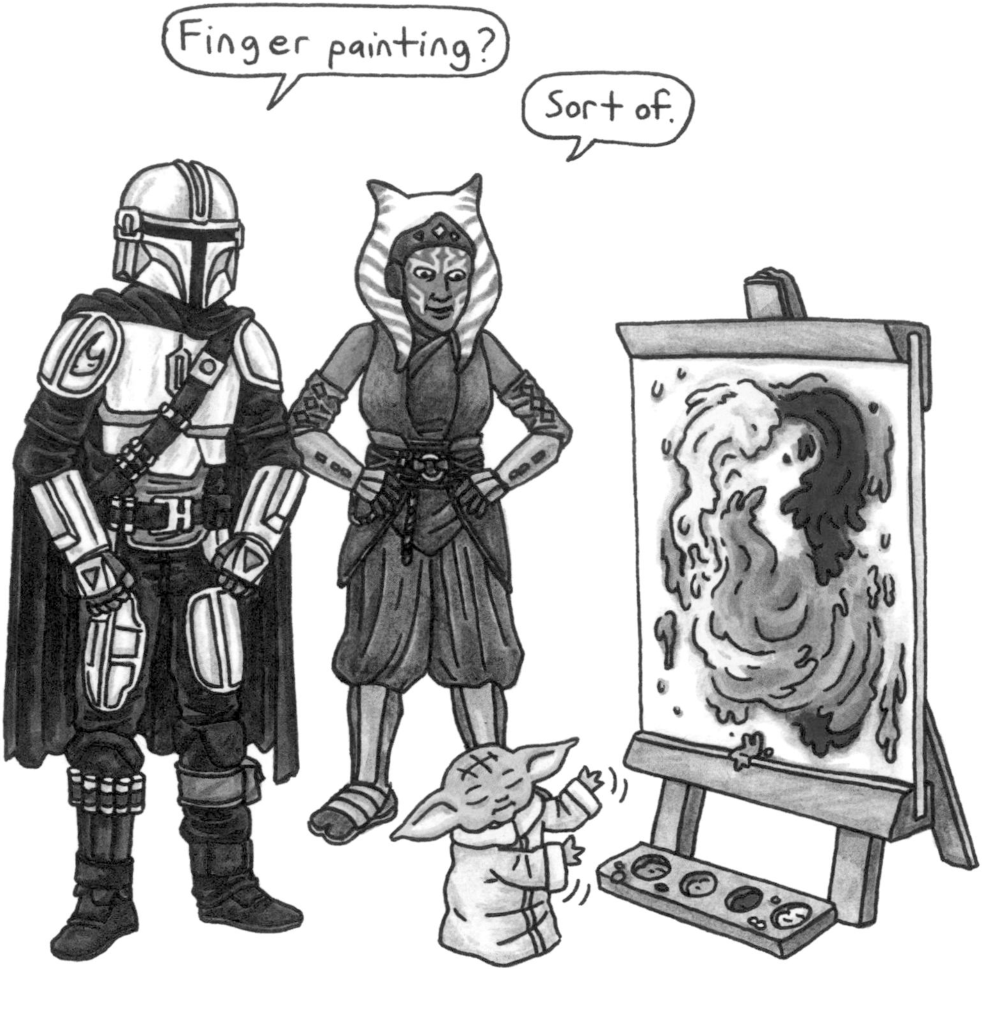
Finger painting?
Sort of.

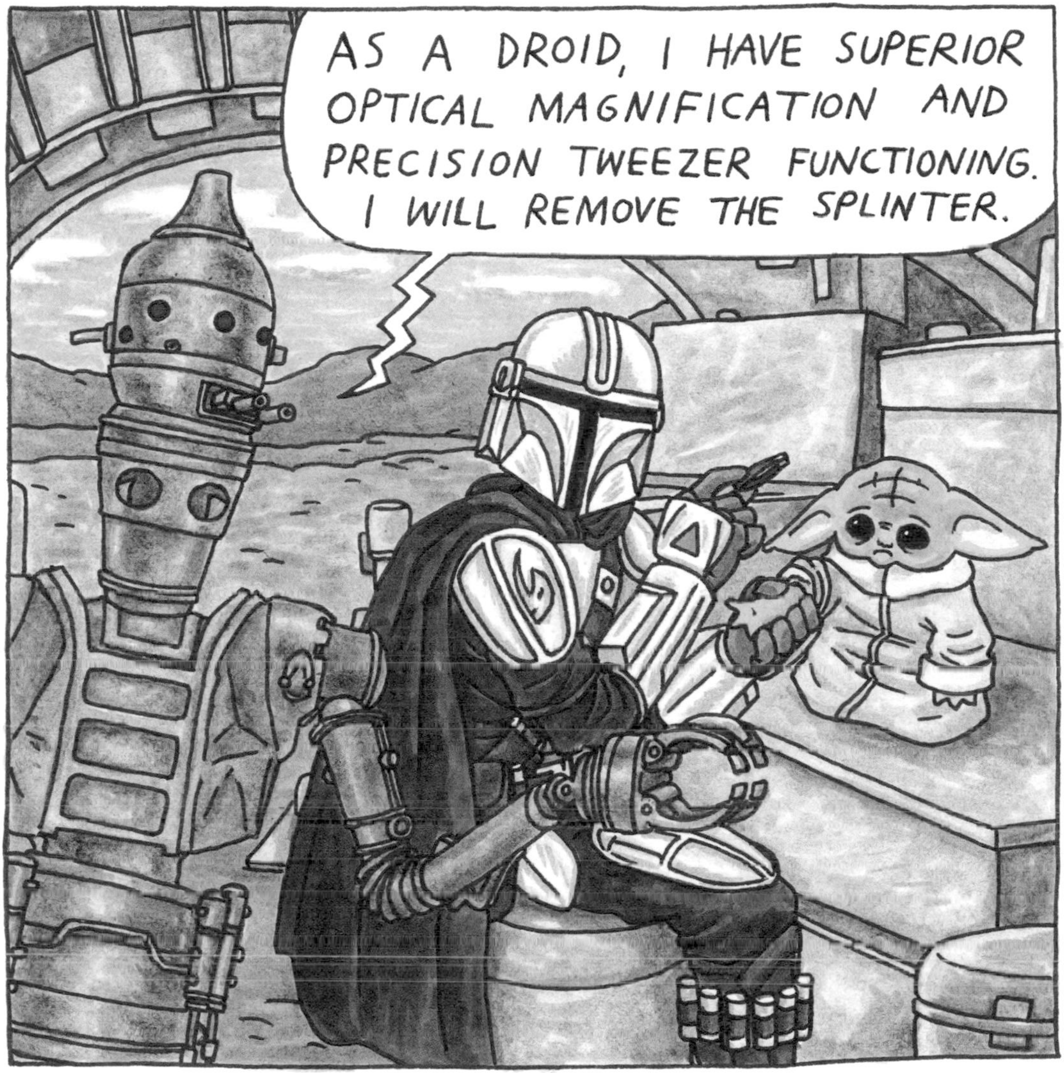
AS A DROID, I HAVE SUPERIOR OPTICAL MAGNIFICATION AND PRECISION TWEEZER FUNCTIONING. I WILL REMOVE THE SPLINTER.

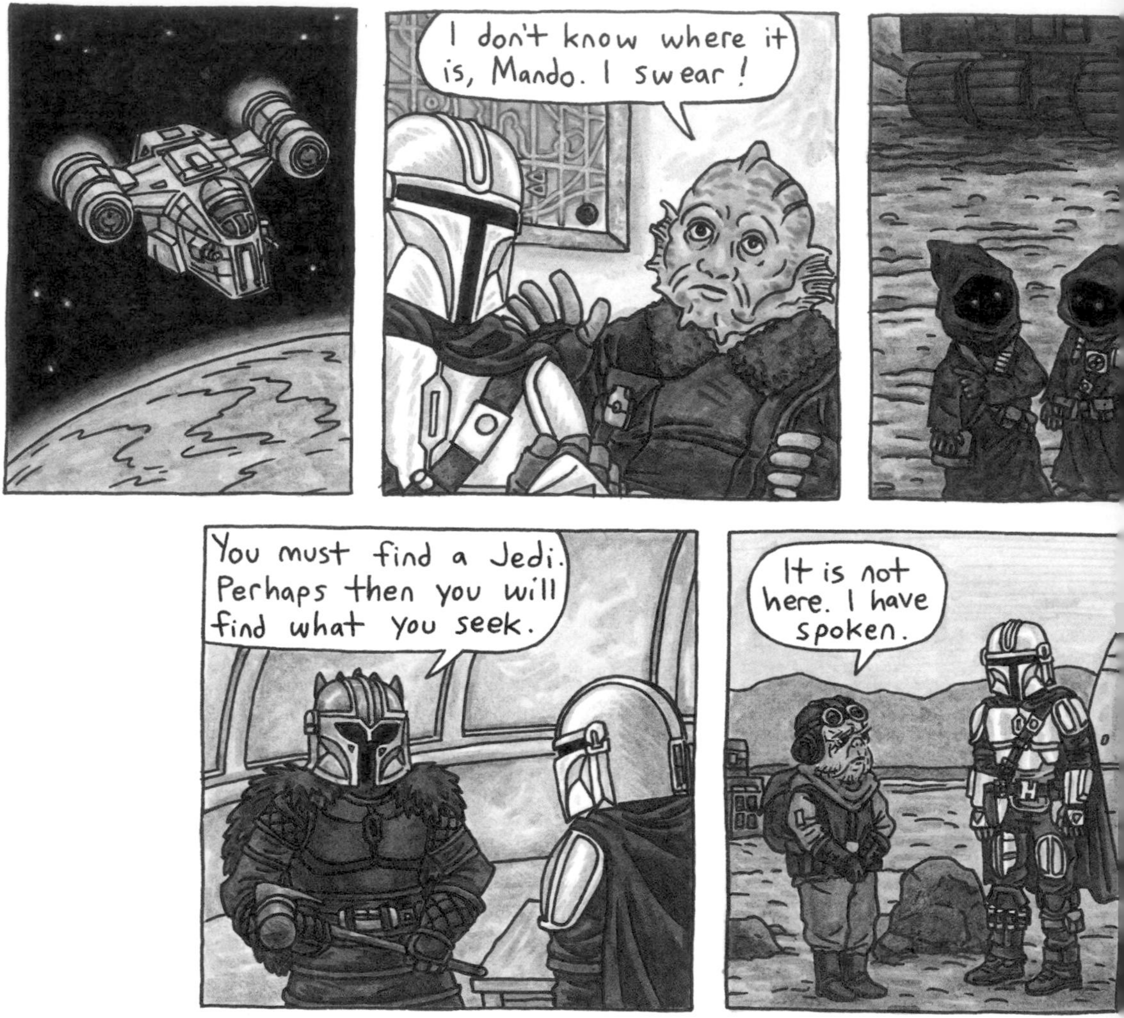
I don't know where it is, Mando. I swear!
You must find a Jedi. Perhaps then you will find what you seek.
It is not here. I have spoken.

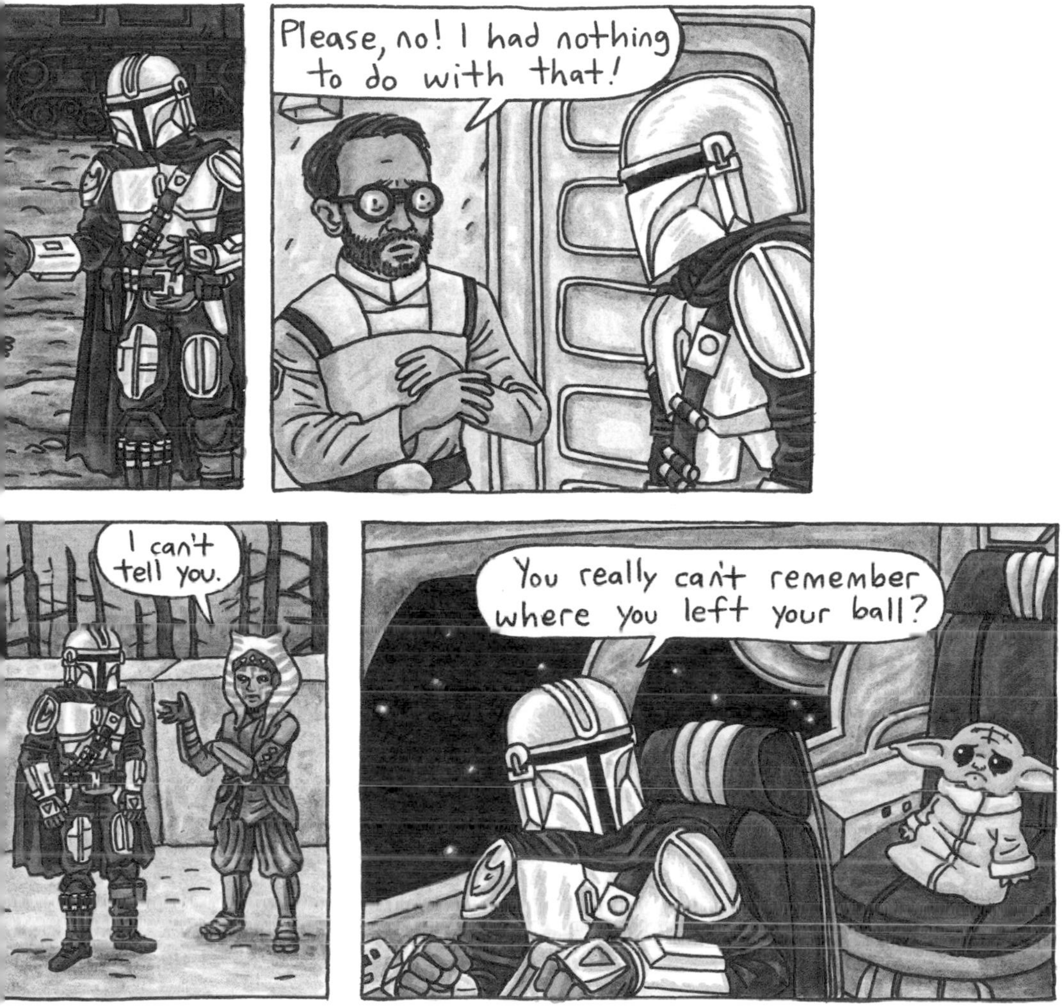
Please, no! I had nothing to do with that!
I can't tell you.
You really can't remember where you left your ball?

Oh, you got a bad boo-boo, didn't you? Yes, you did. I know. It's okay...
You need to start spending more time around adults, Mando.

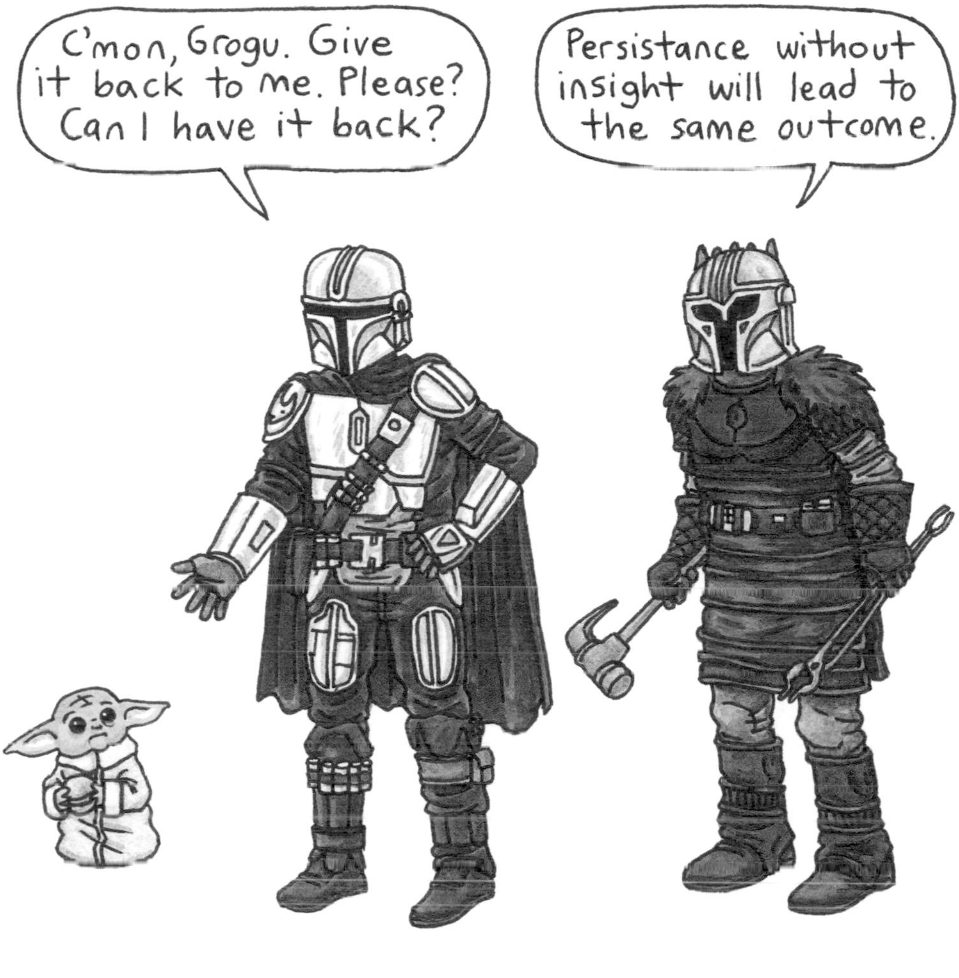
C'mon, Grogu. Give it back to me. Please? Can I have it back?
Persistance without insight will lead to the same outcome.

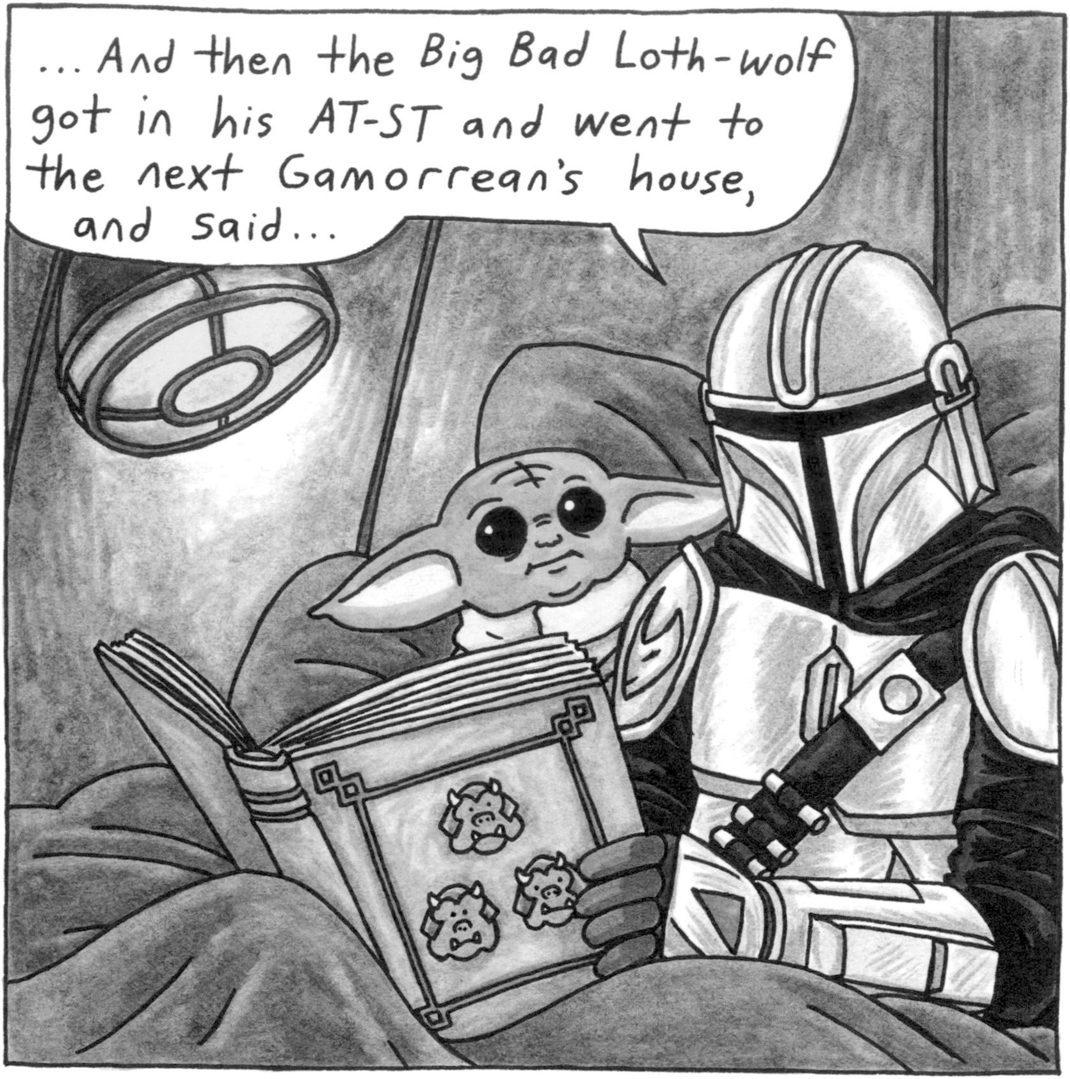
...And then the Big Bad Loth-wolf got in his AT-ST and went to the next Gamorrean's house, and said...

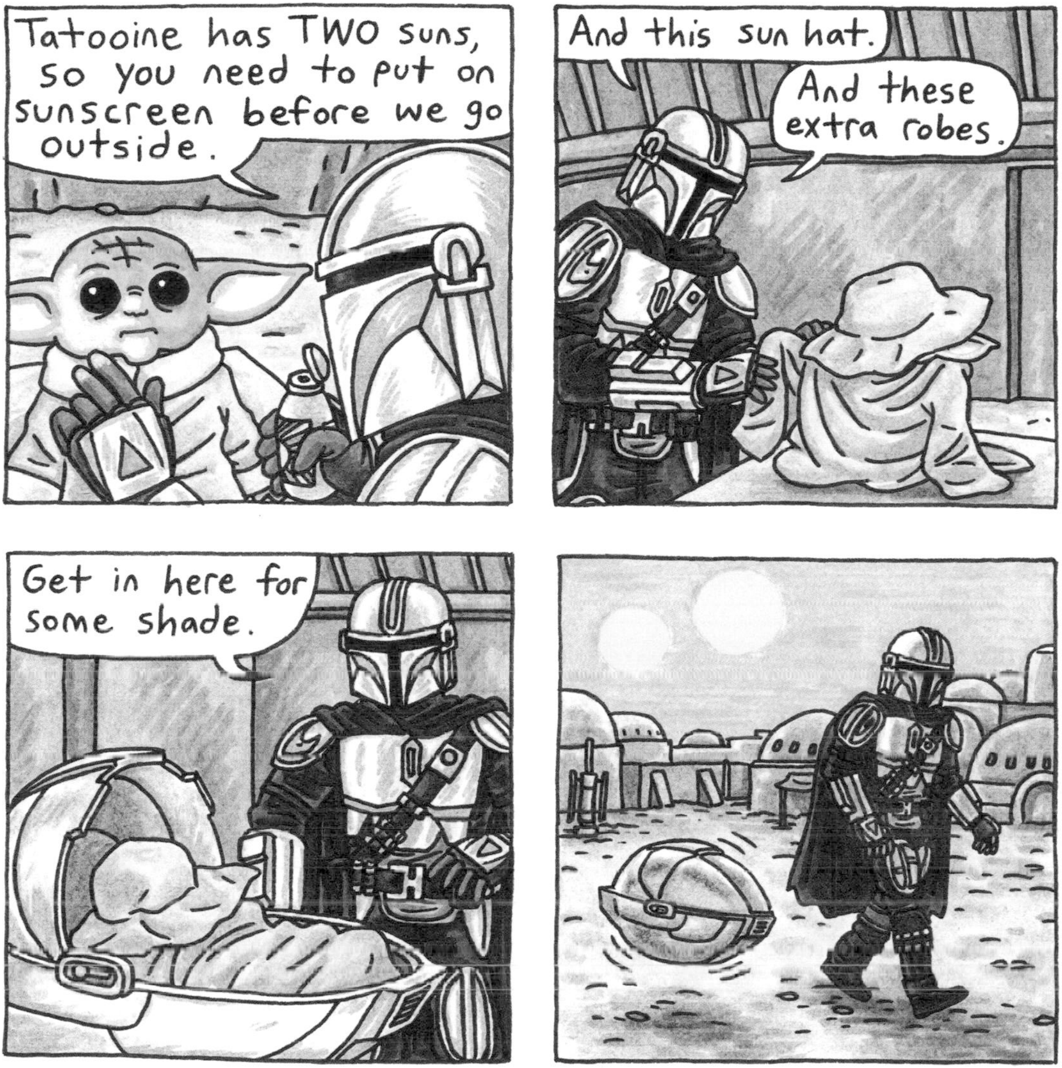
Tatooine has TWO suns, so you need to put on sunscreen before we go outside.
And this sun hat.
And these extra robes.
Get in here for some shade.

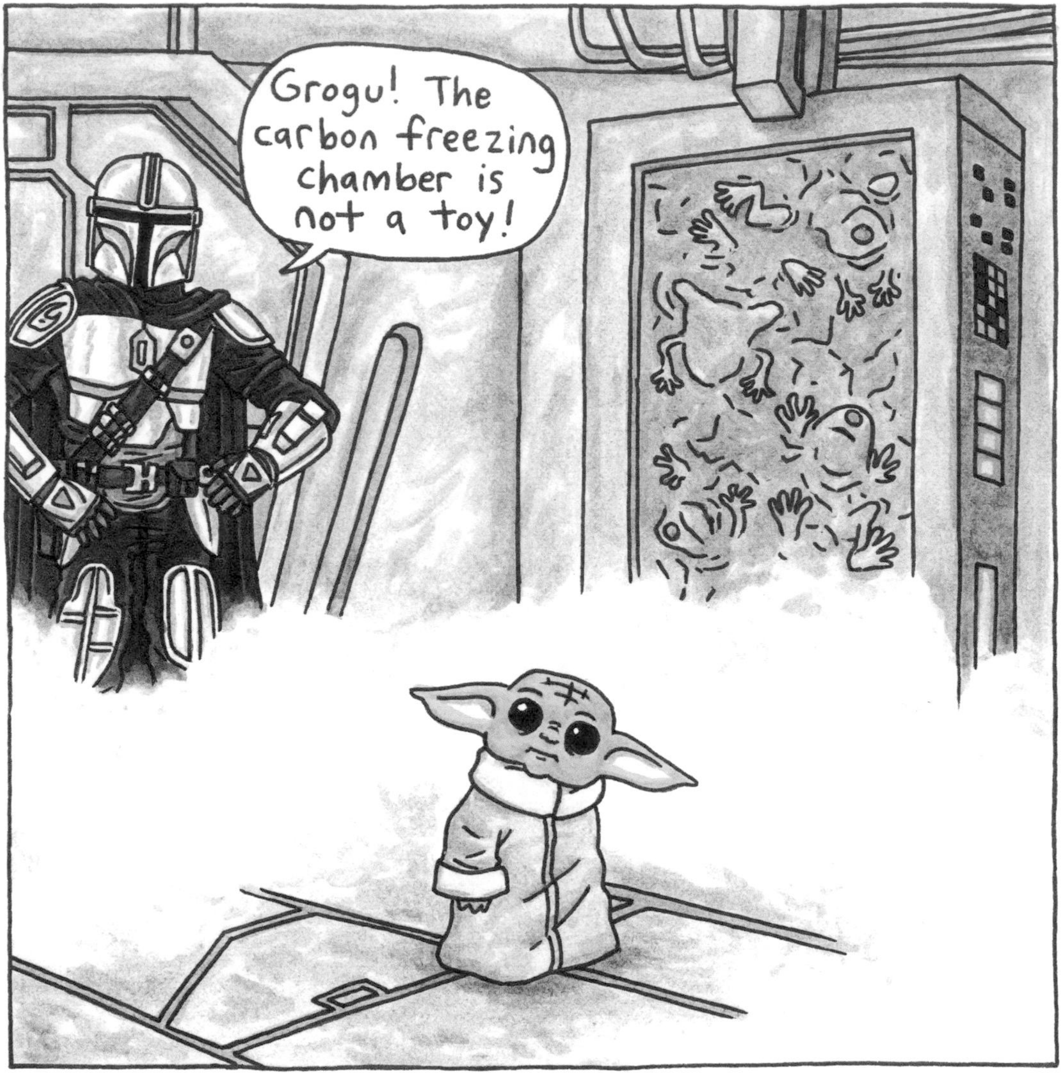
Grogu! The carbon freezing chamber is not a toy!

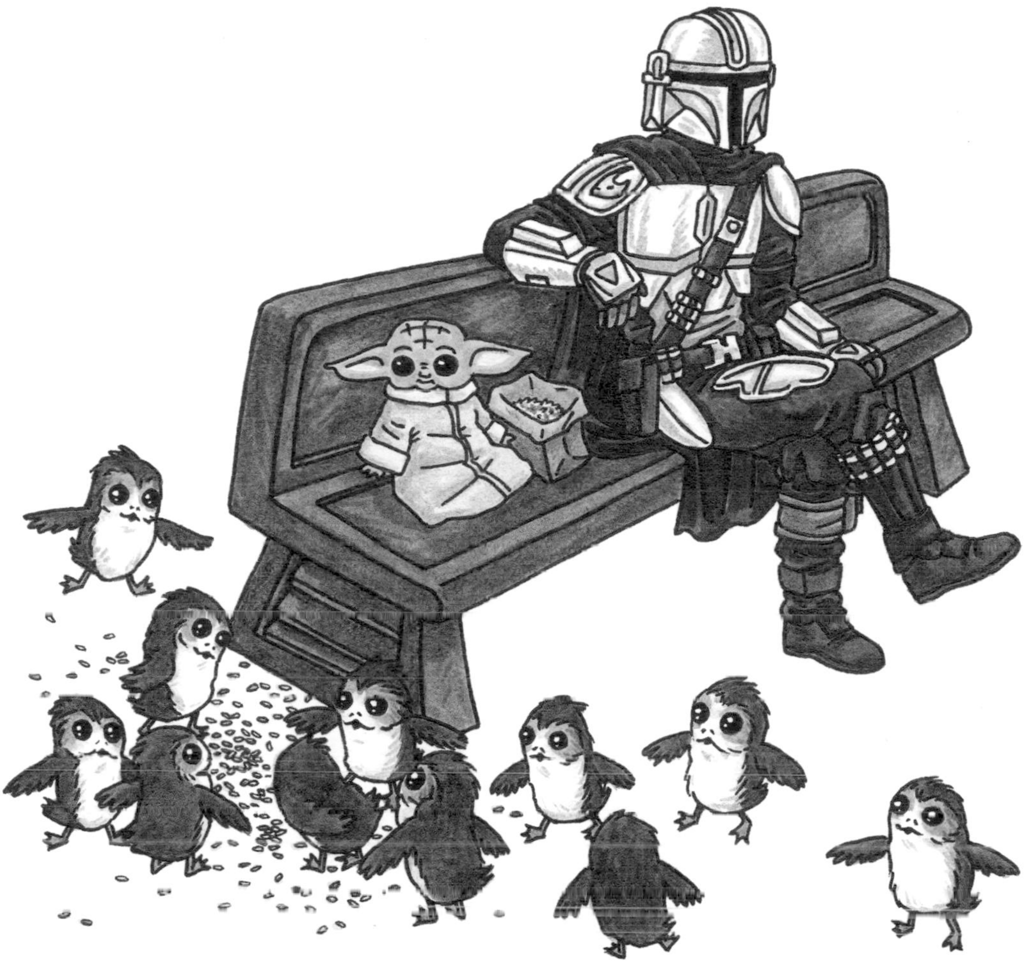

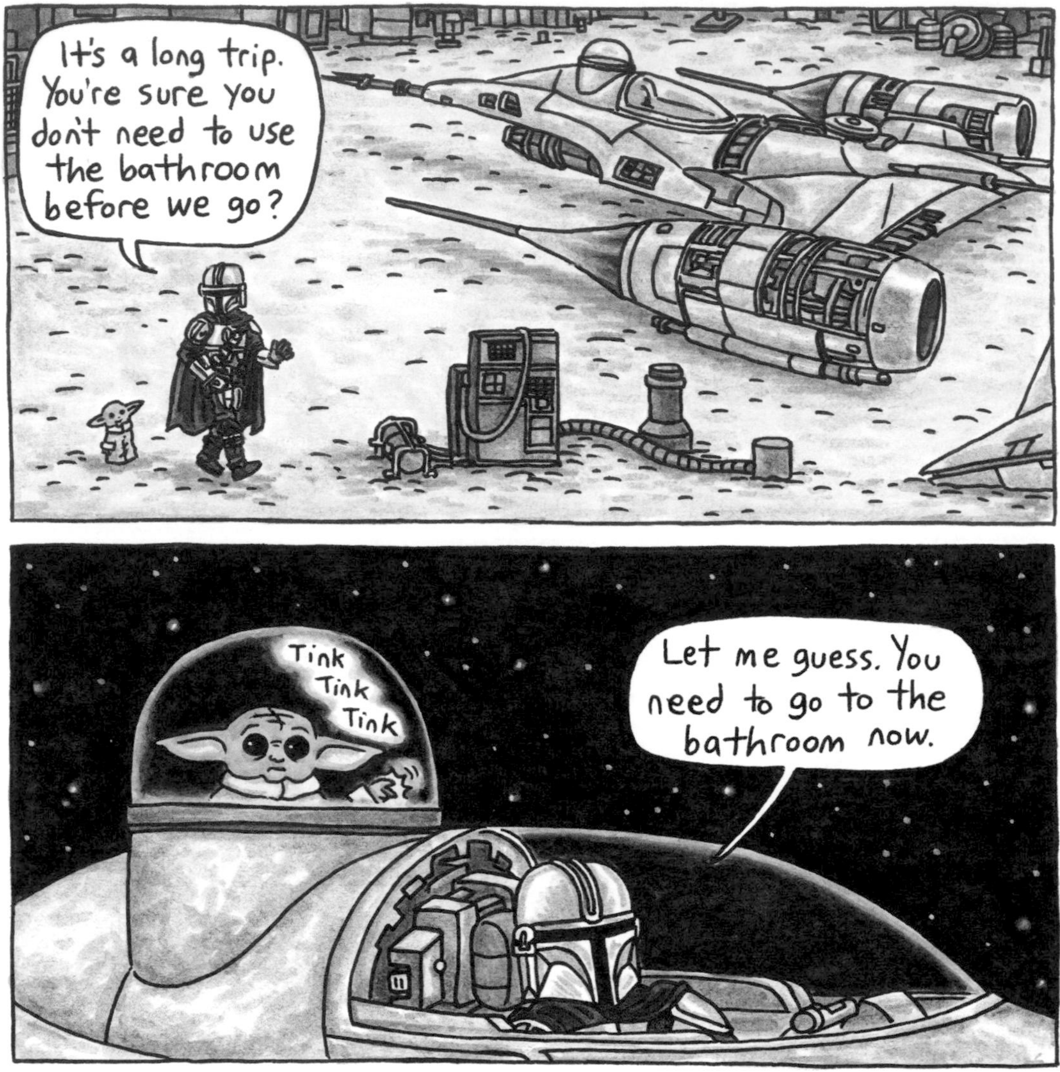
It's a long trip. You're sure you don't need to use the bathroom before we go?
Tink
Tink
Tink
Let me guess. You need to go to the bathroom now.

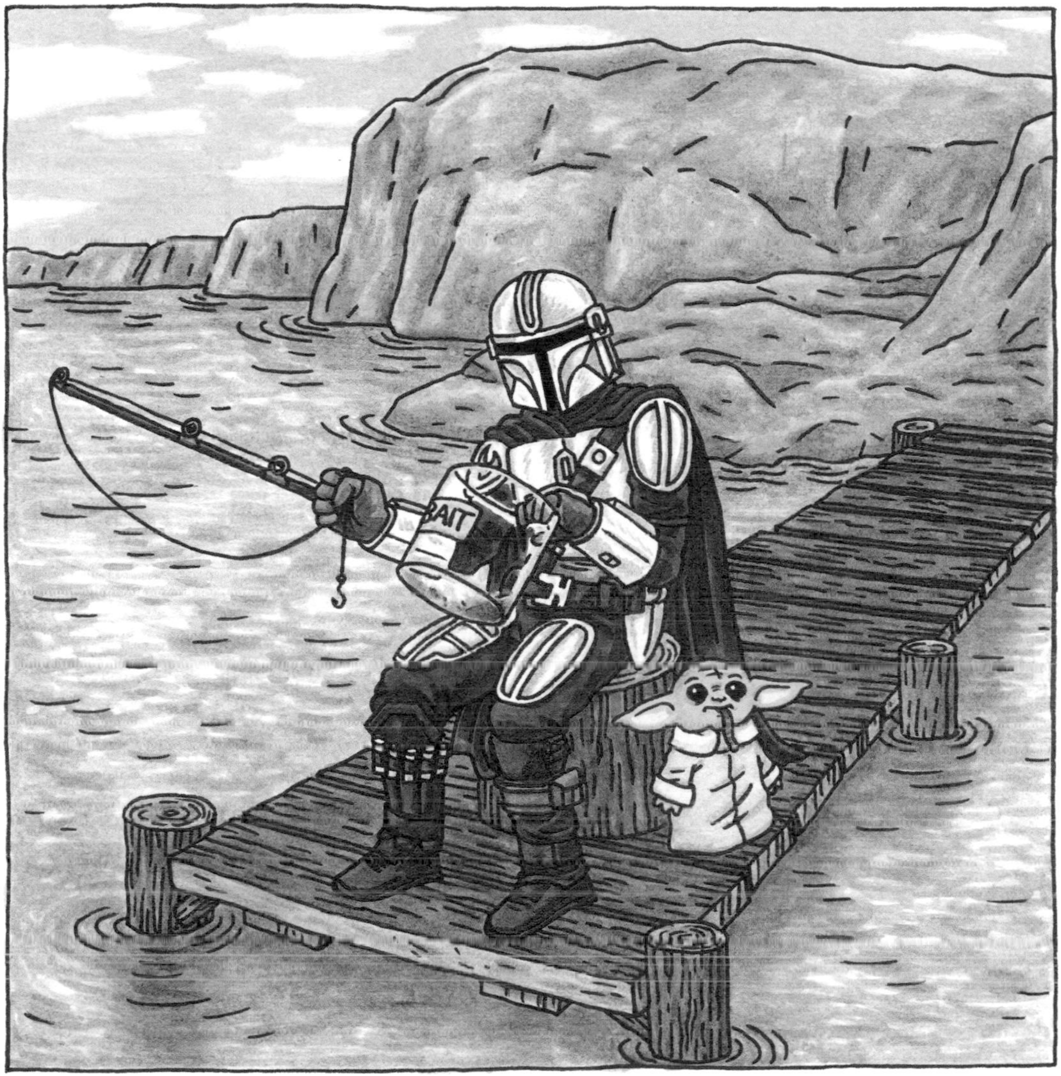
BAIT

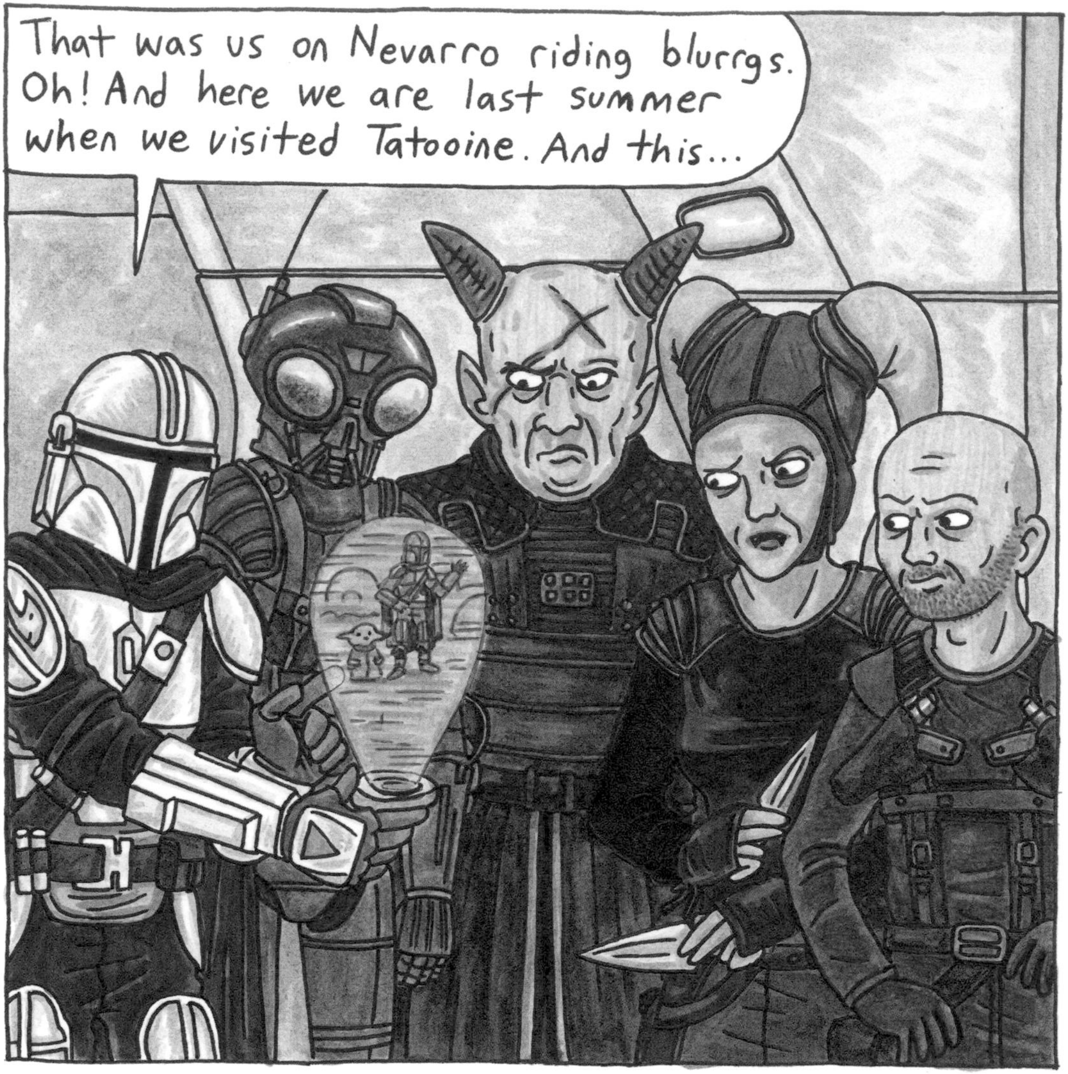
That was us on Nevarro riding blurrgs. Oh! And here we are last summer when we visited Tatooine. And this...

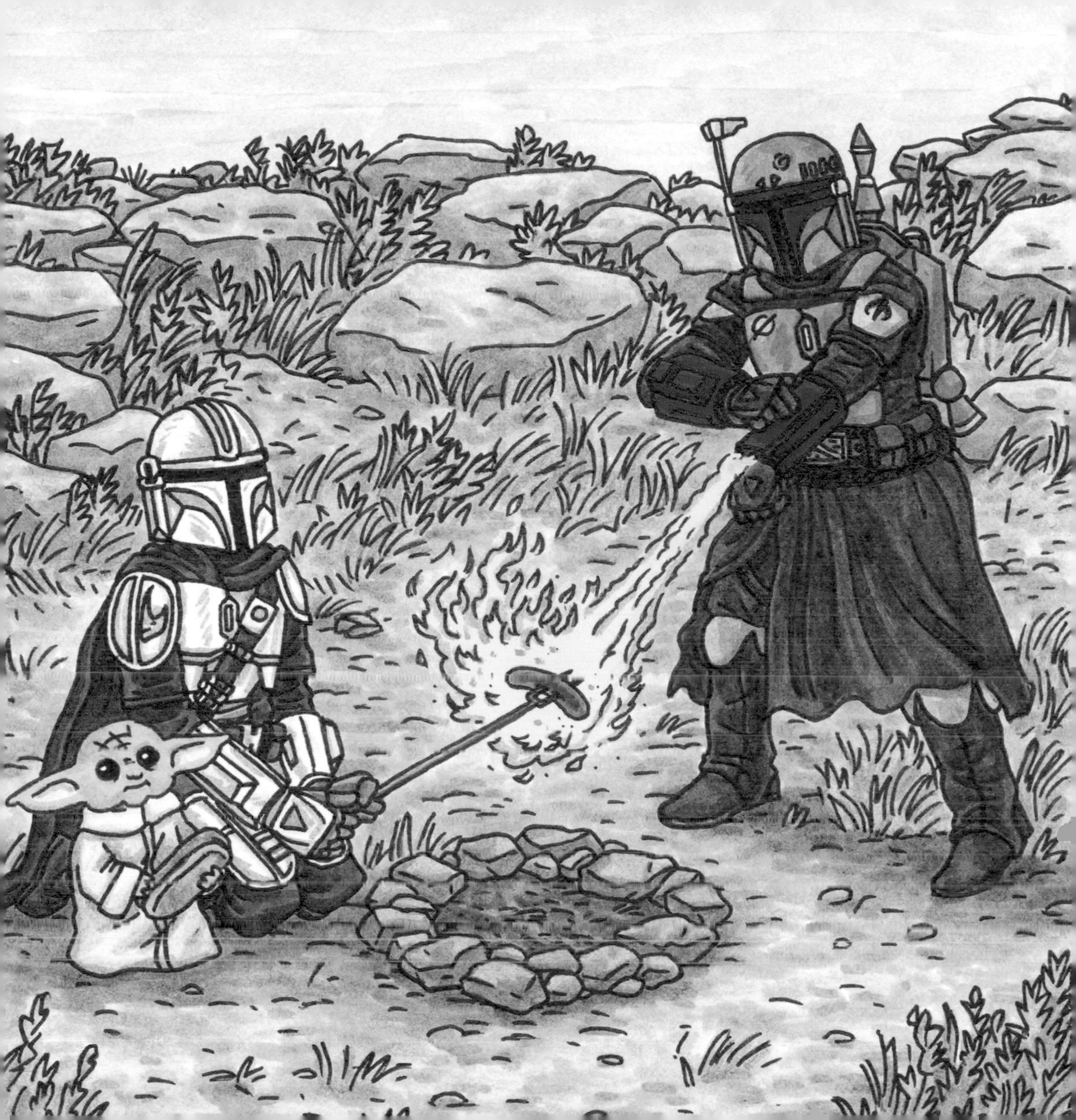

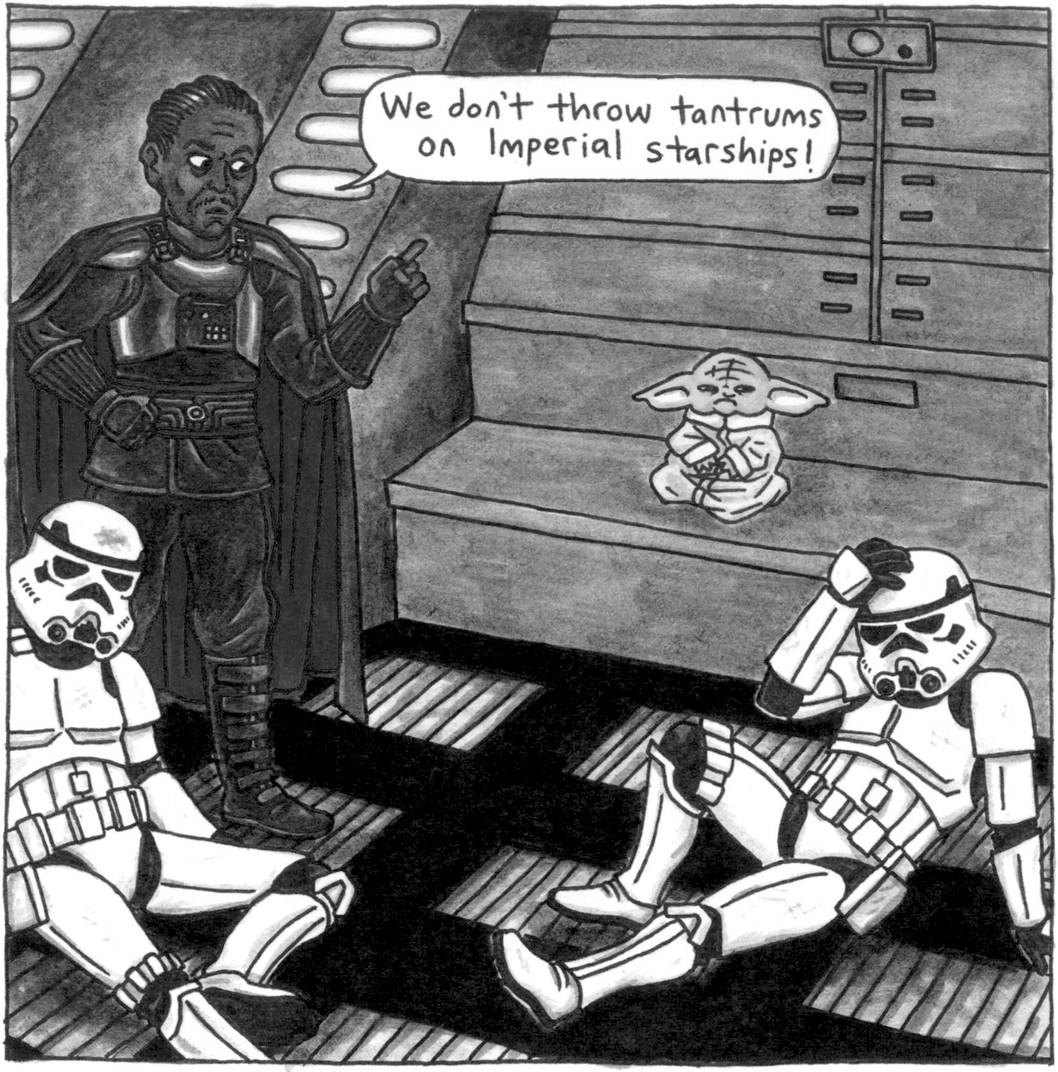
We don't throw tantrums on Imperial starships!

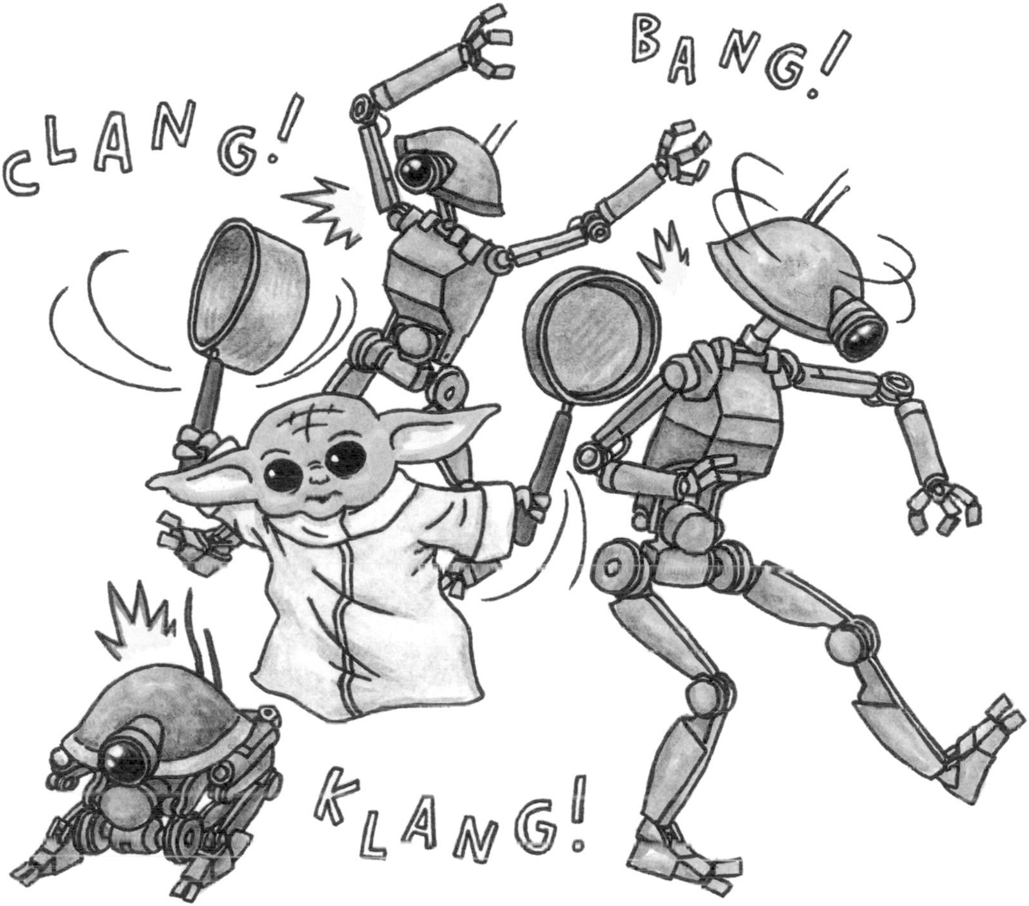
CLANG!
BANG!
KLANG!

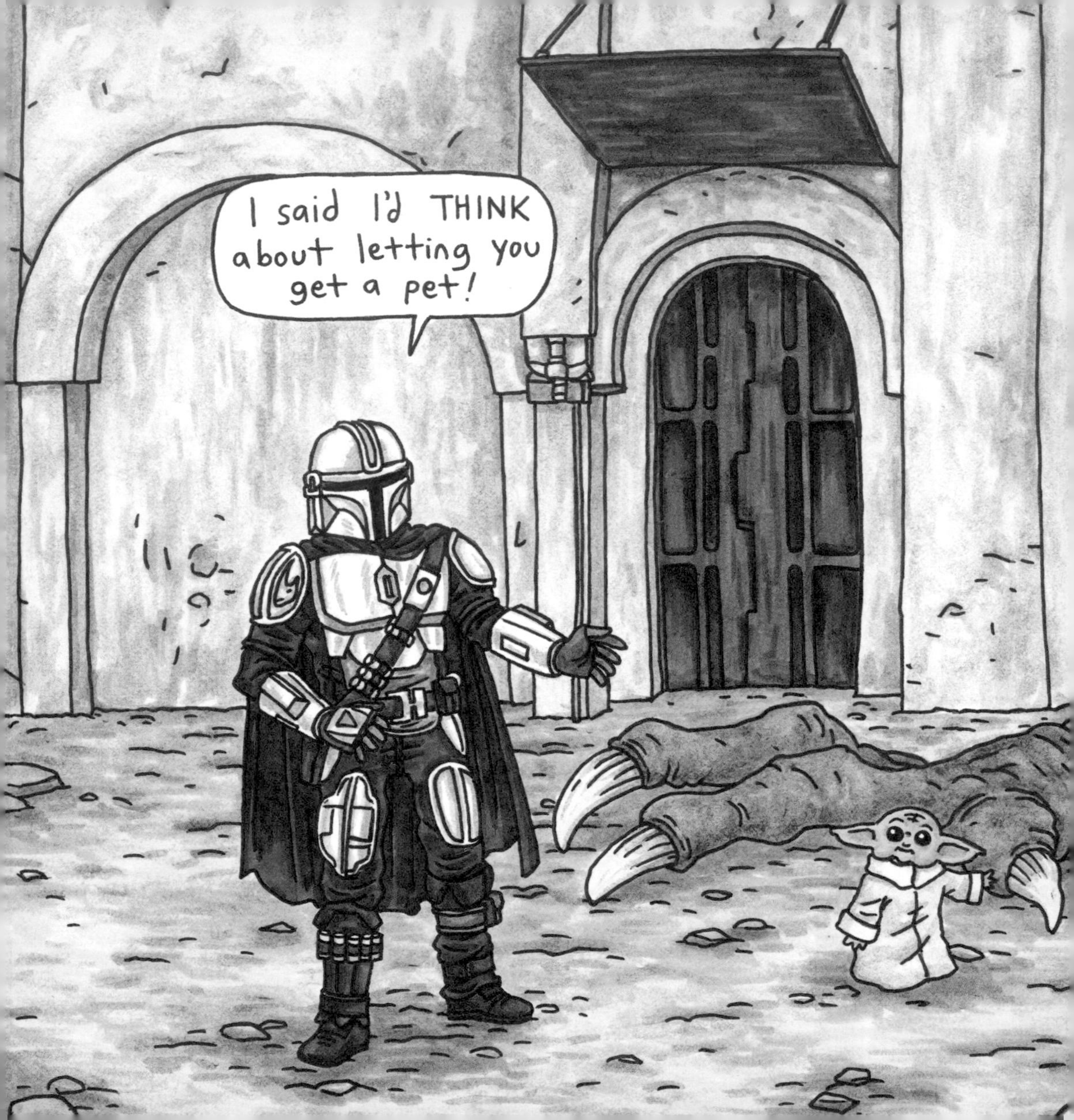
I said I'd THINK about letting you get a pet!

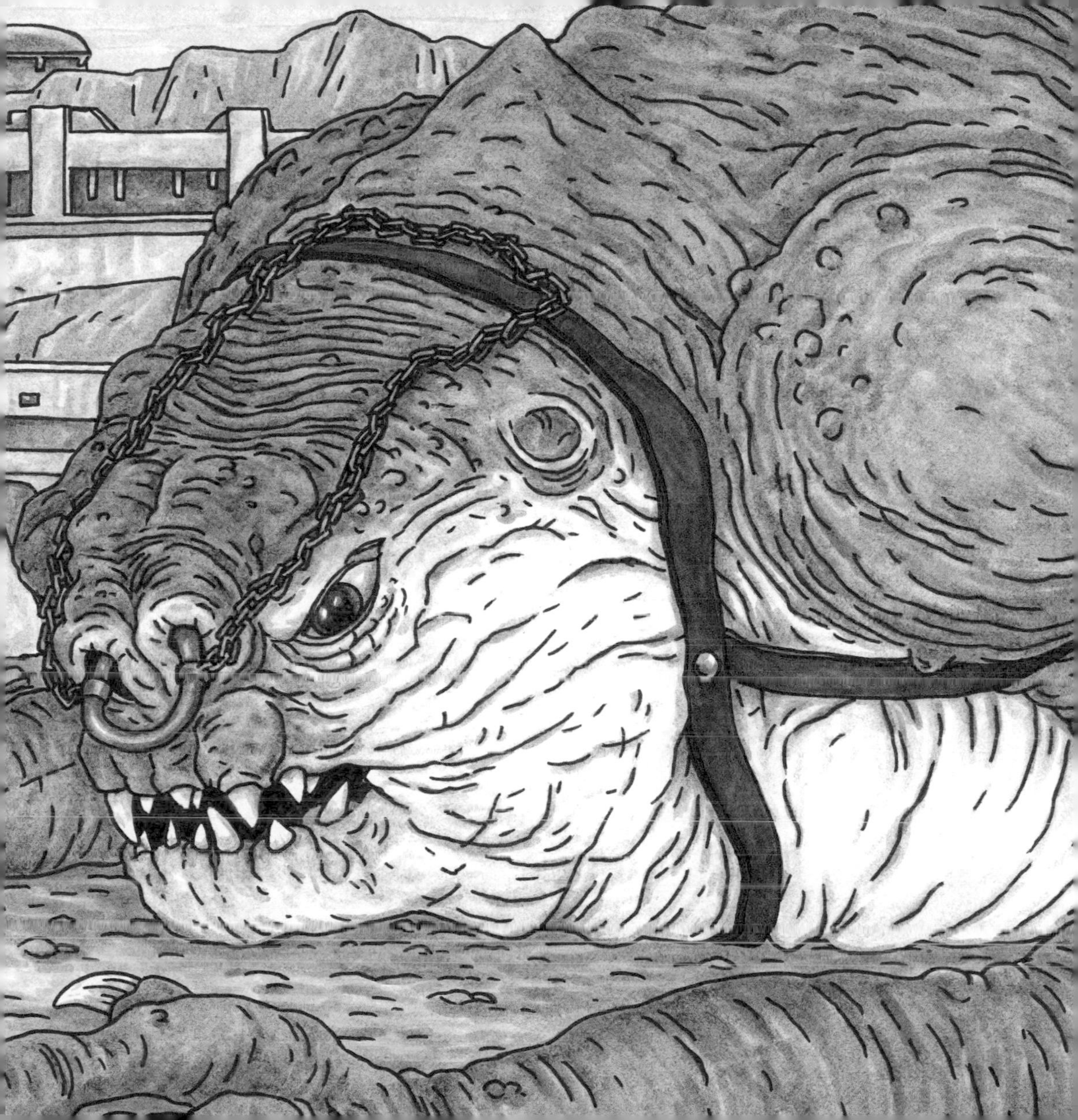

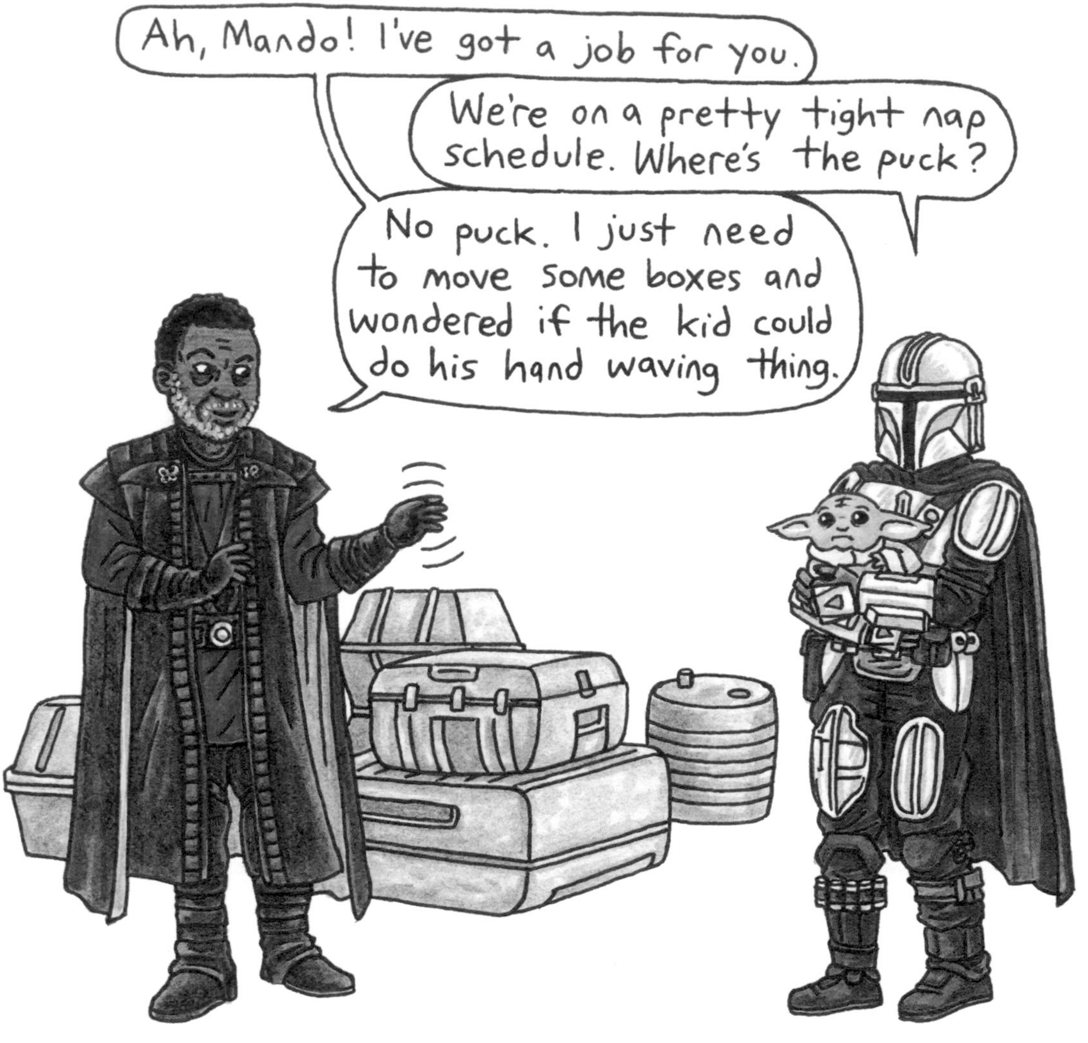
Ah, Mando! I've got a job for you.
We're on a pretty tight nap schedule. Where's the puck?
No puck. I just need to move some boxes and wondered if the kid could do his hand waving thing.

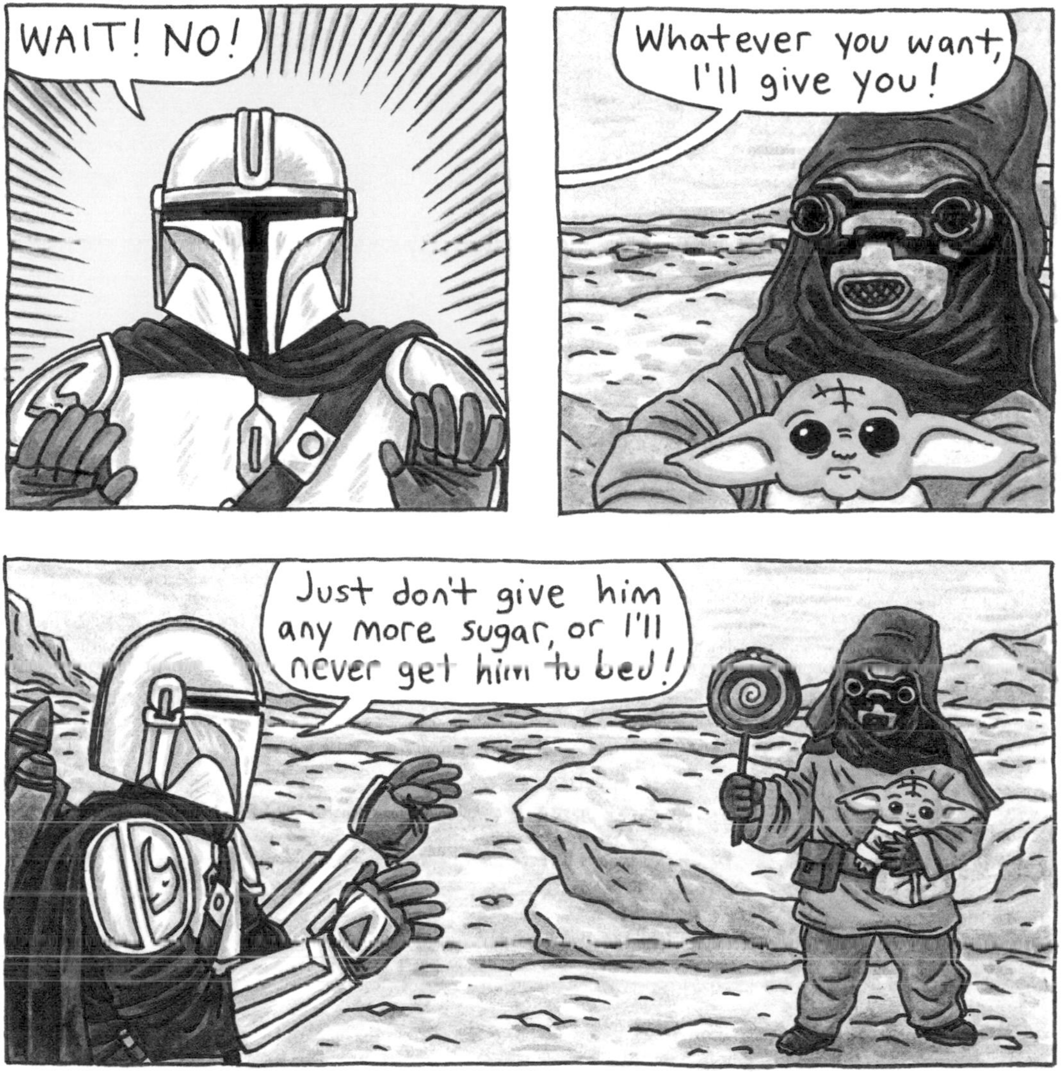
WAIT! NO!
Whatever you want, I'll give you!
Just don't give him any more sugar, or I'll never get him to bed!

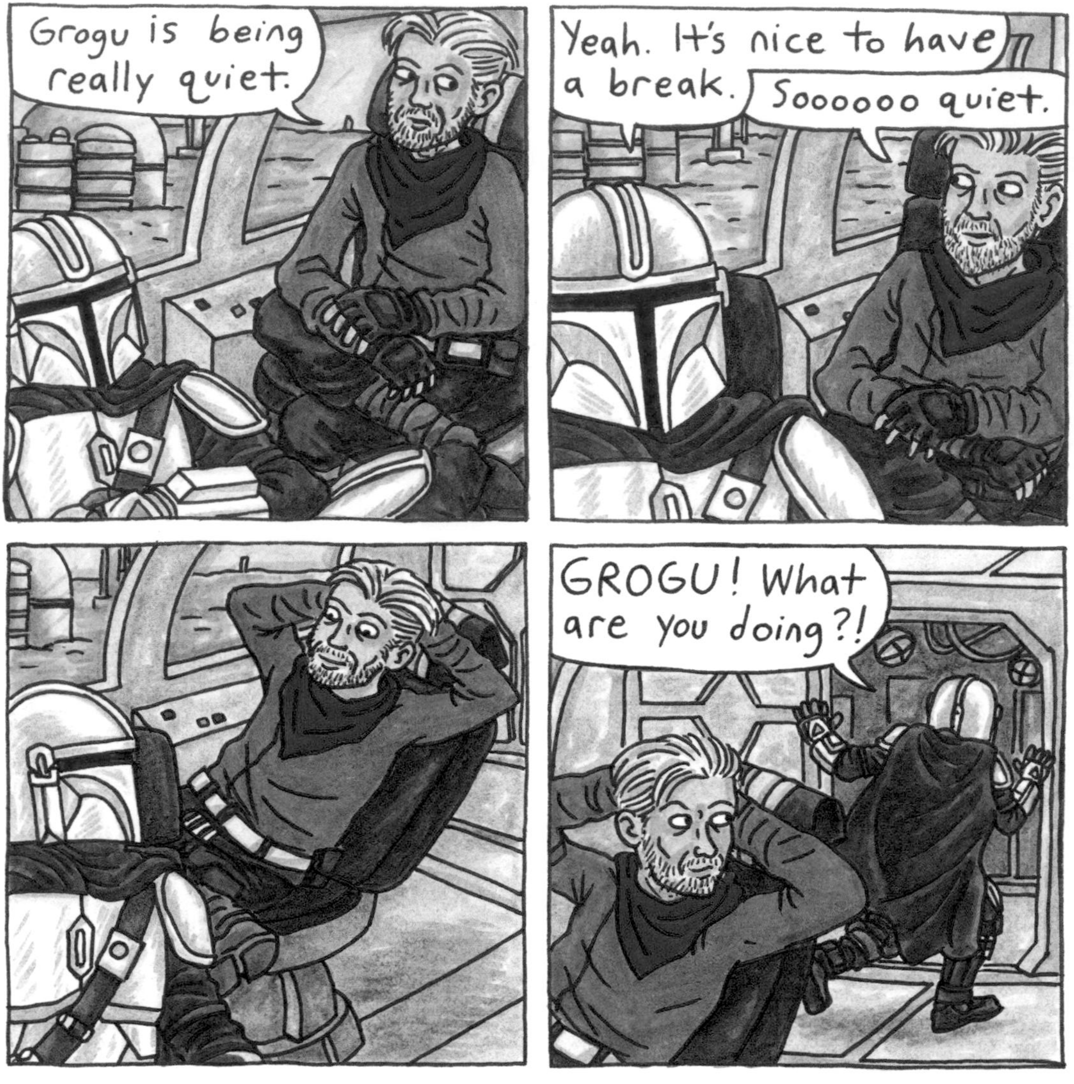
Grogu is being really quiet.
Yeah. It's nice to have a break.
Soooooo quiet.
GROGU! What are you doing?!

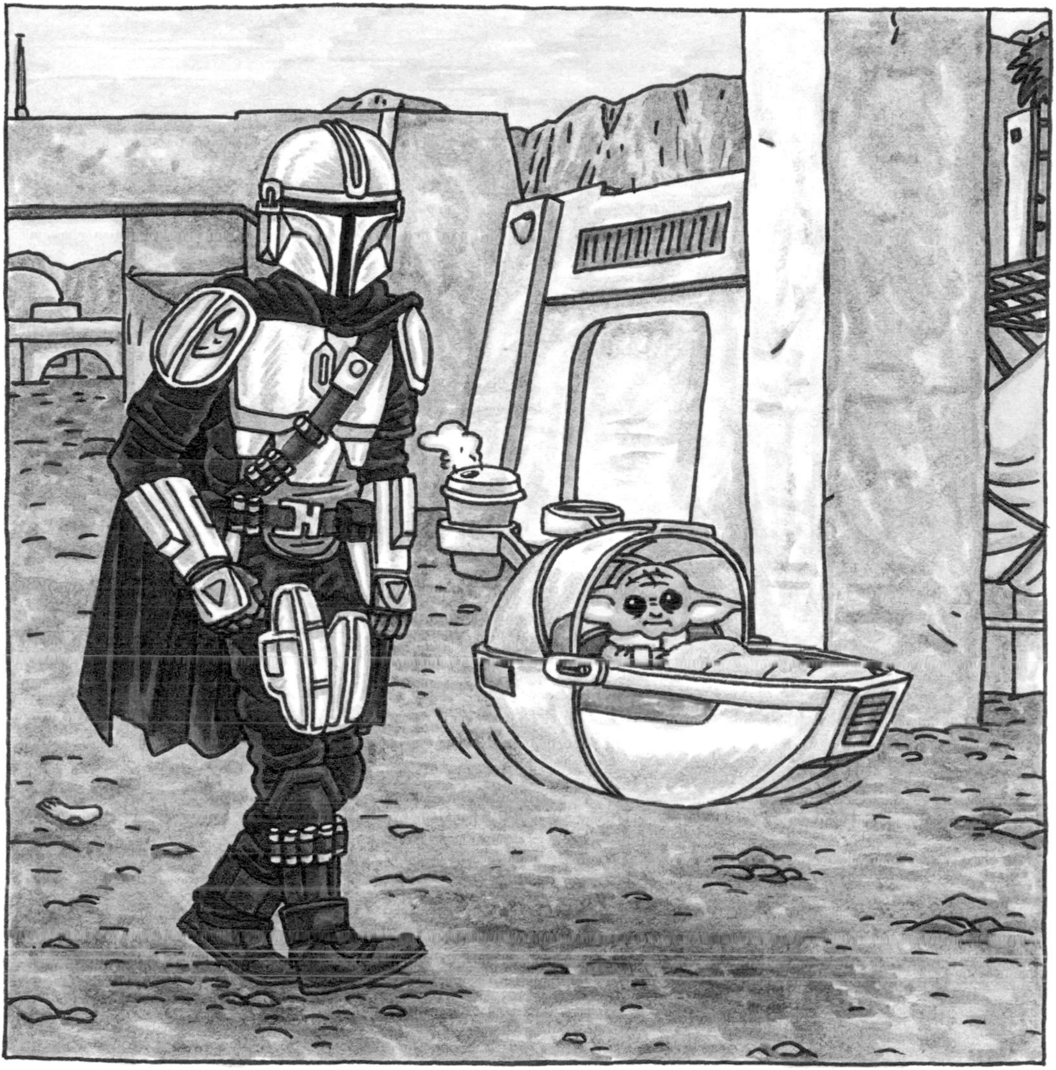

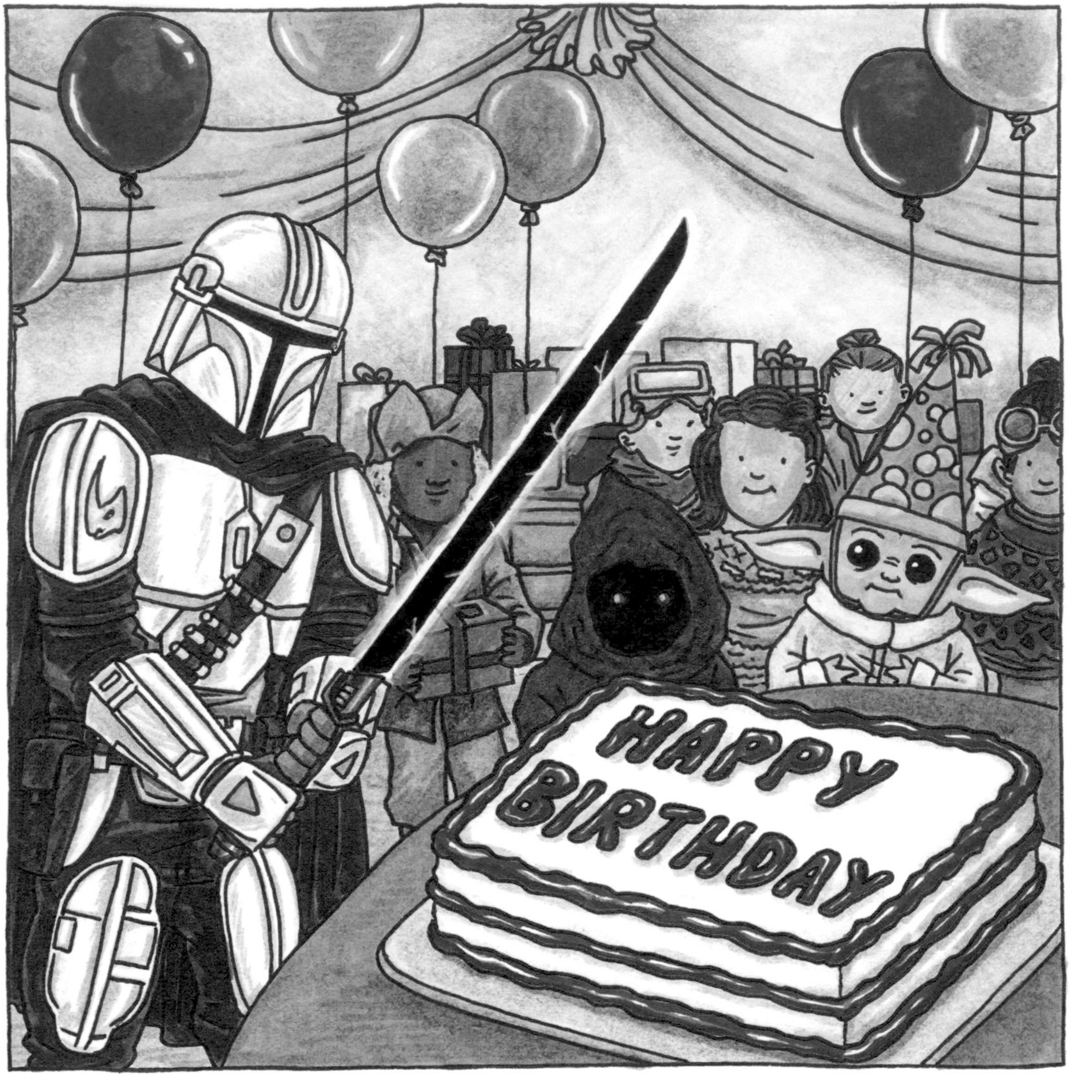
HAPPY
BIRTHDAY

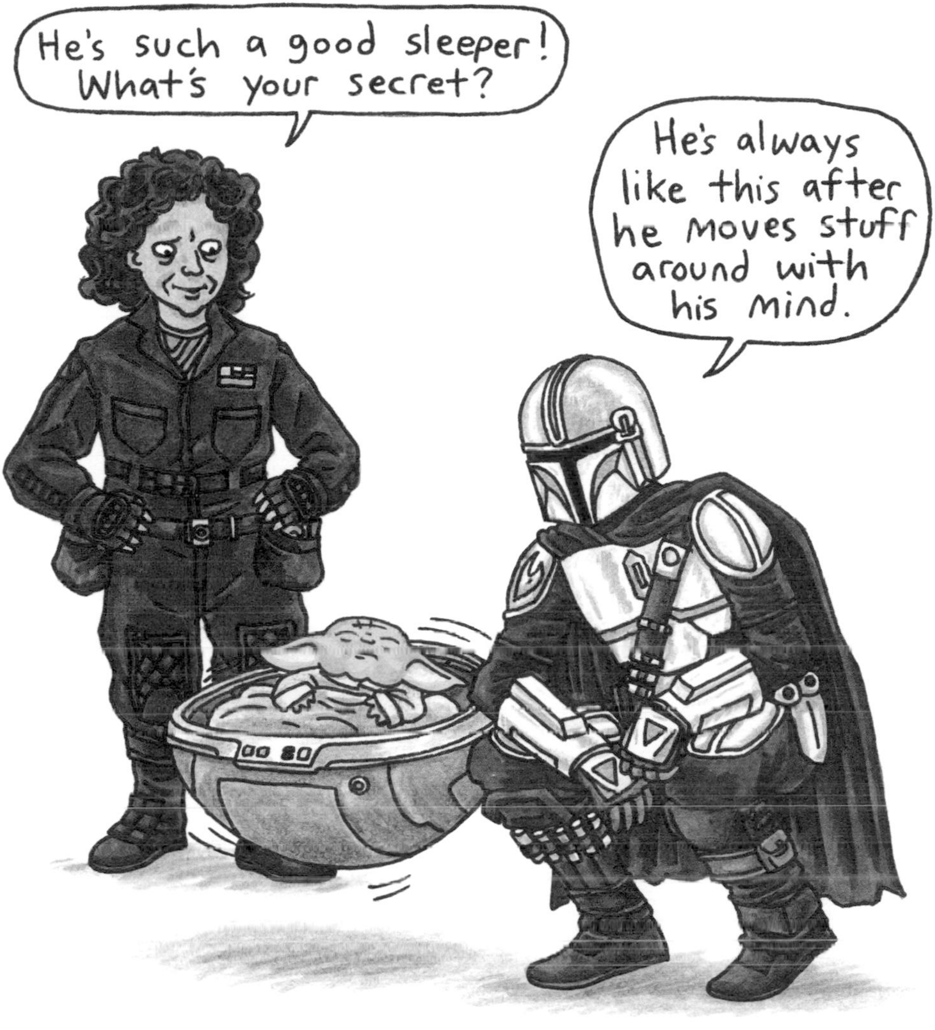
He's such a good sleeper! What's your secret?
He's always like this after he moves stuff around with his mind.

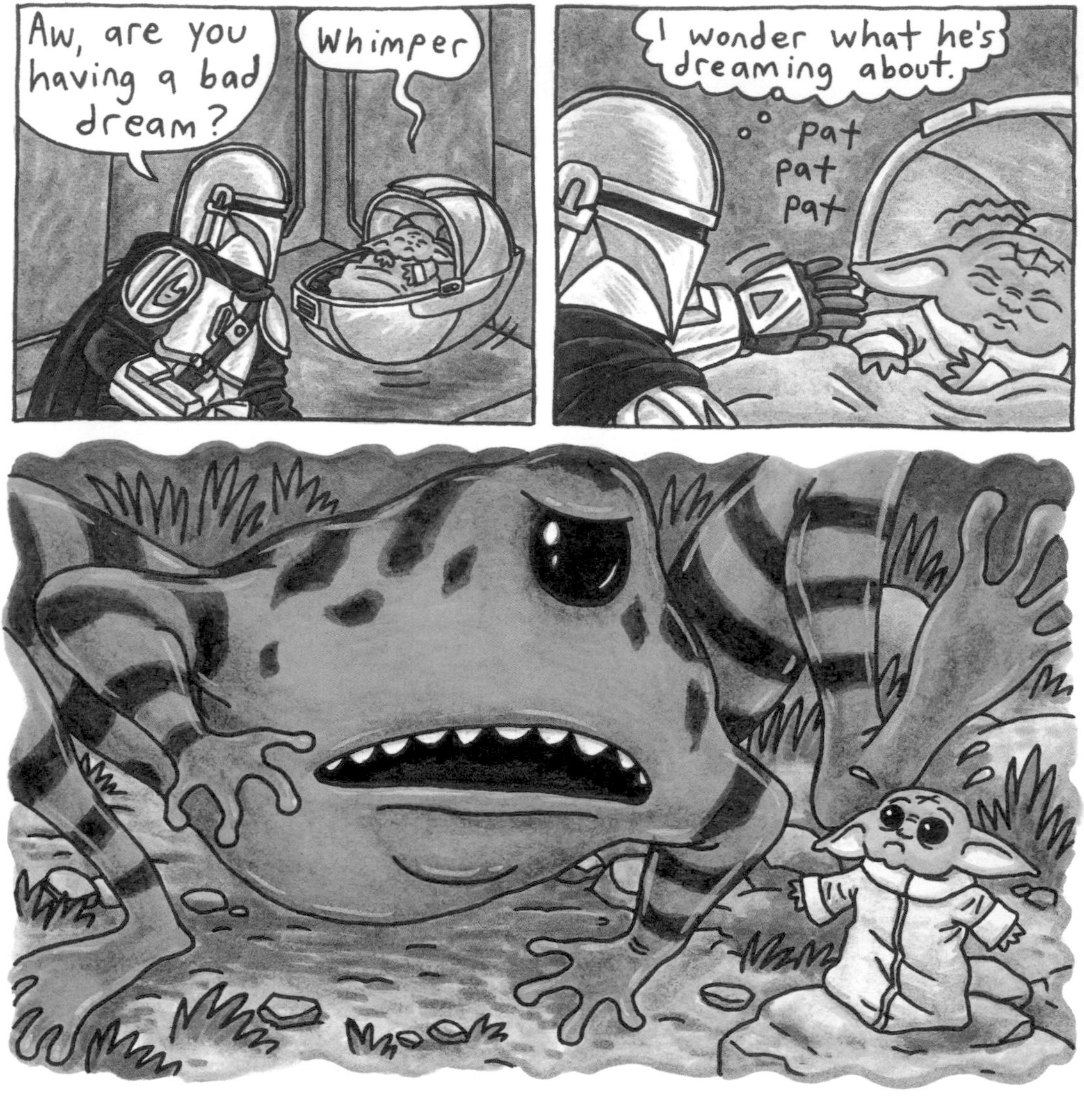
Aw, are you having a bad dream?
Whimper
I wonder what he's dreaming about.
pat pat pat

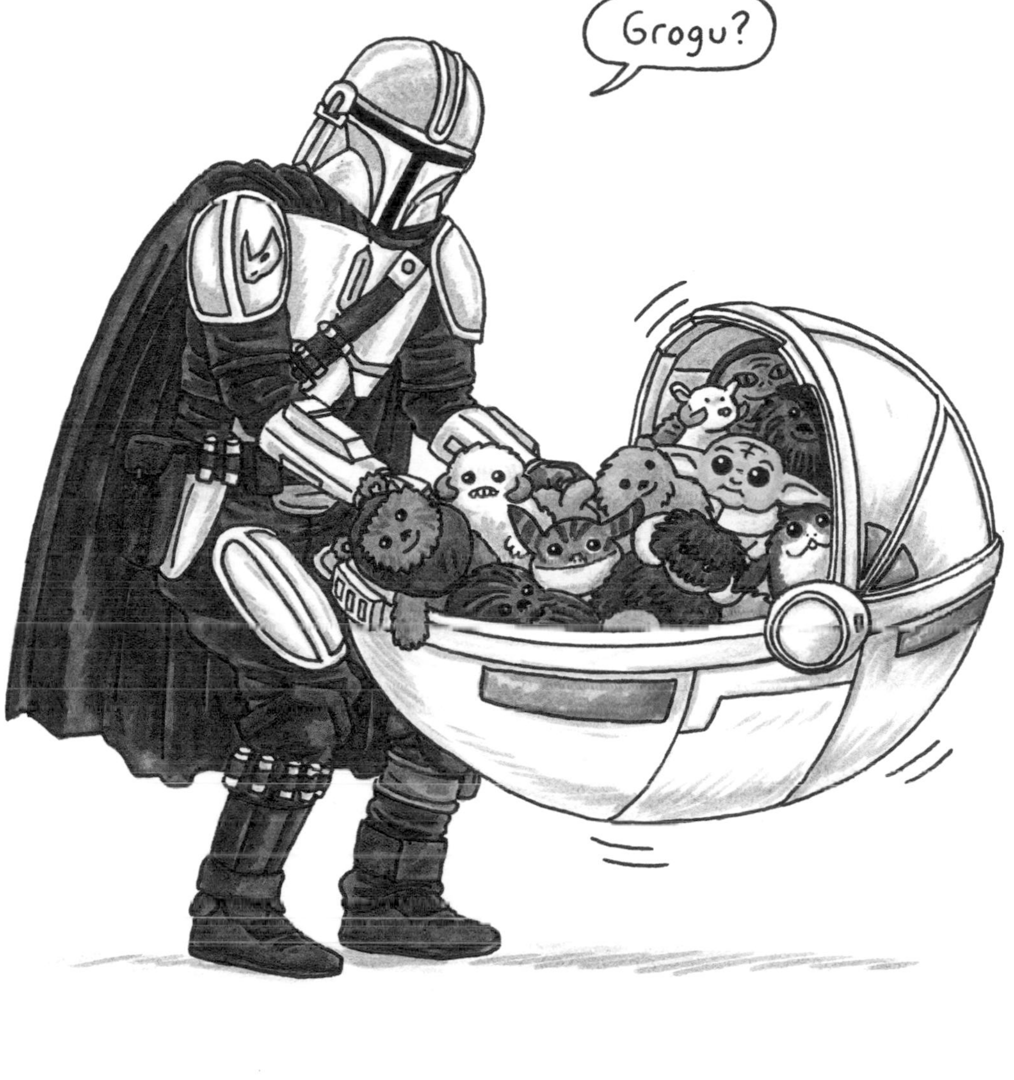
Grogu?

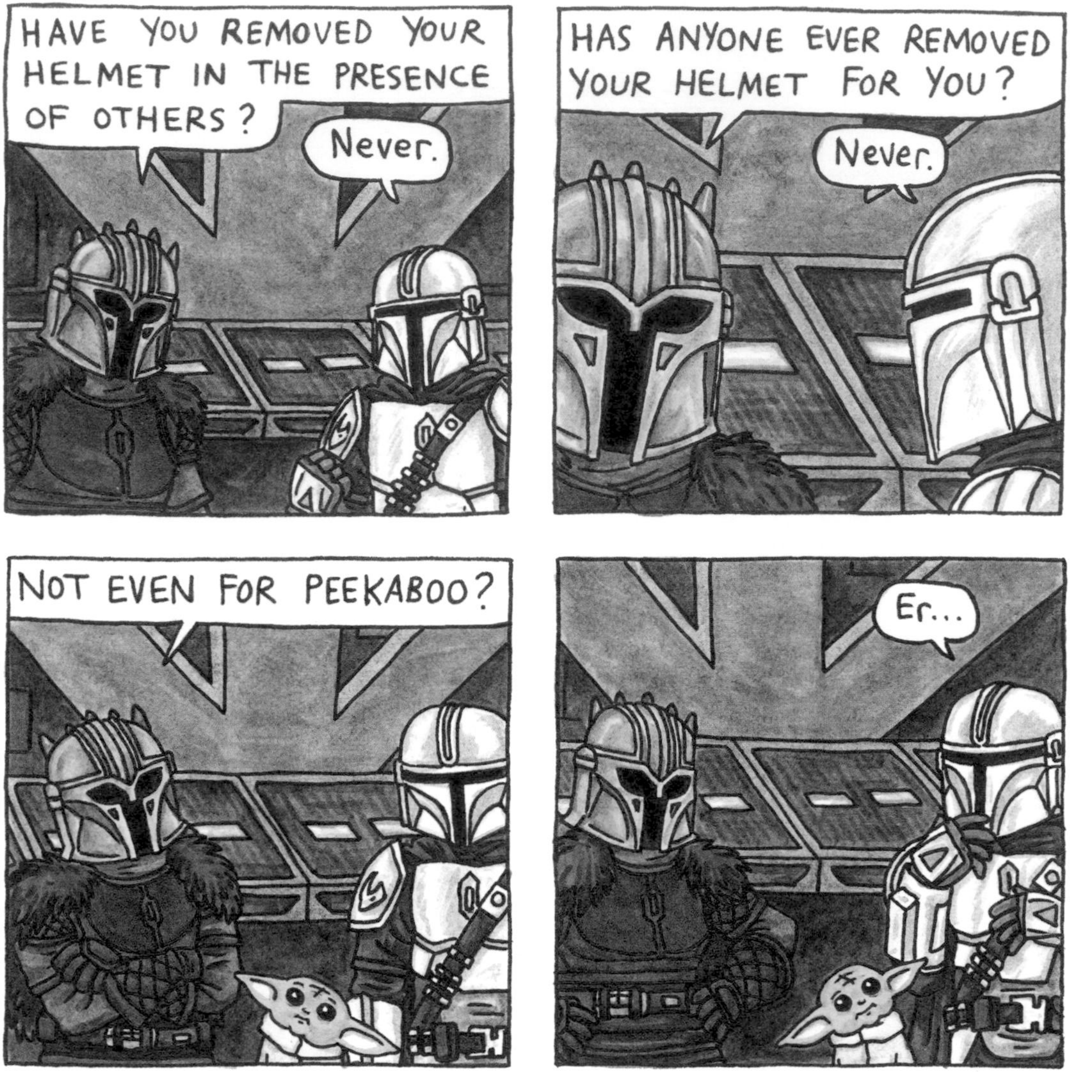
HAVE YOU REMOVED YOUR HELMET IN THE PRESENCE OF OTHERS?
Never.
HAS ANYONE EVER REMOVED YOUR HELMET FOR YOU?
Never.
NOT EVEN FOR PEEKABOO?
Er...

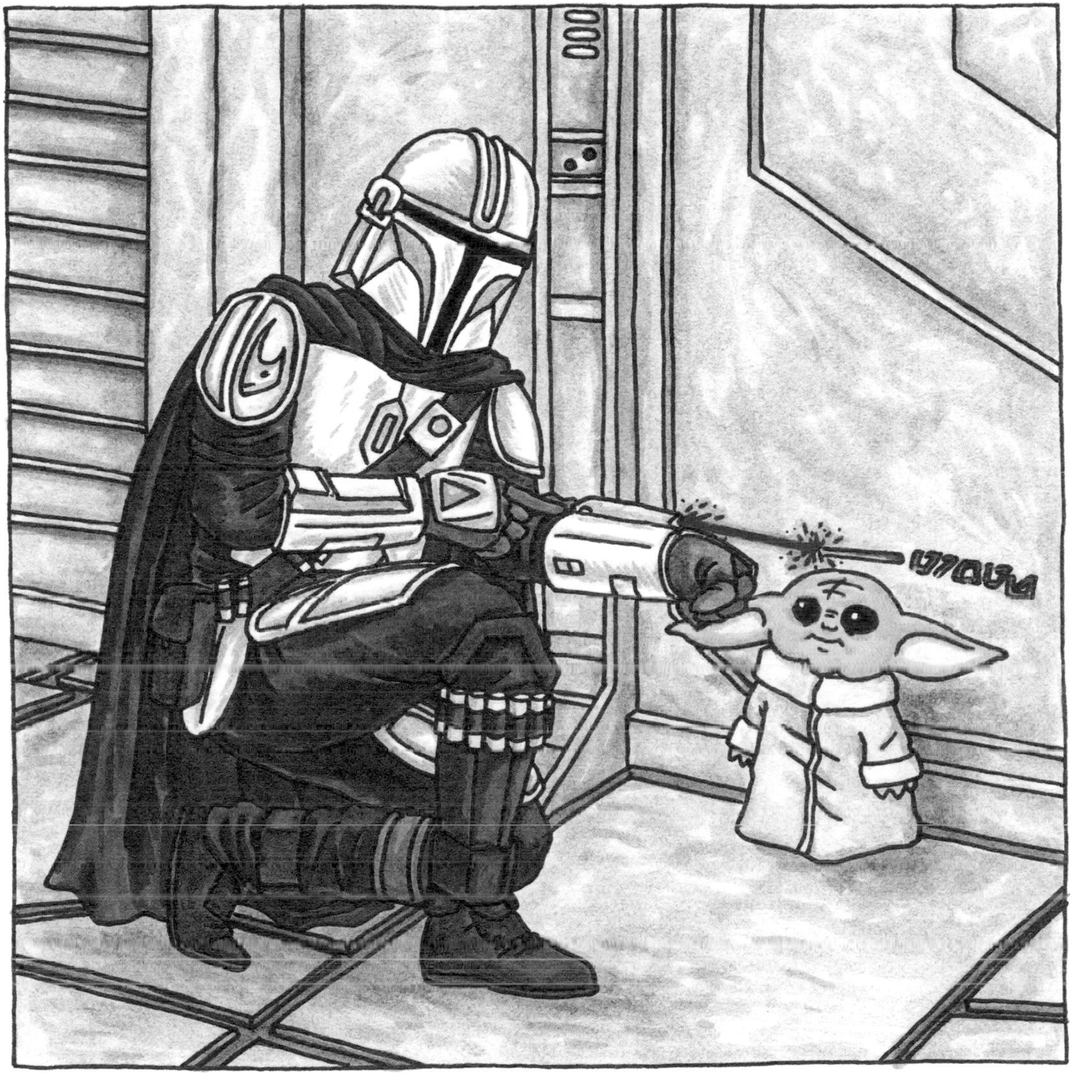

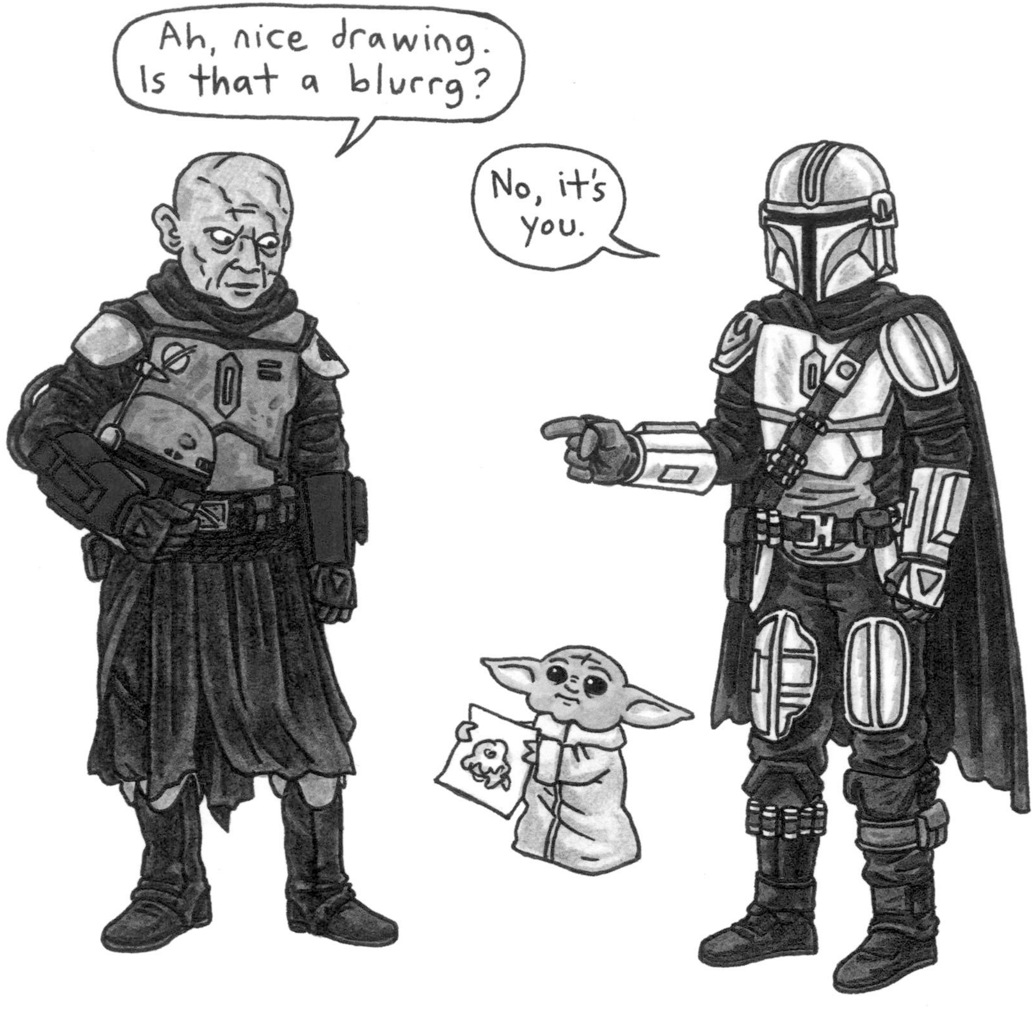
Ah, nice drawing. Is that a blurrg?
No, it's you.

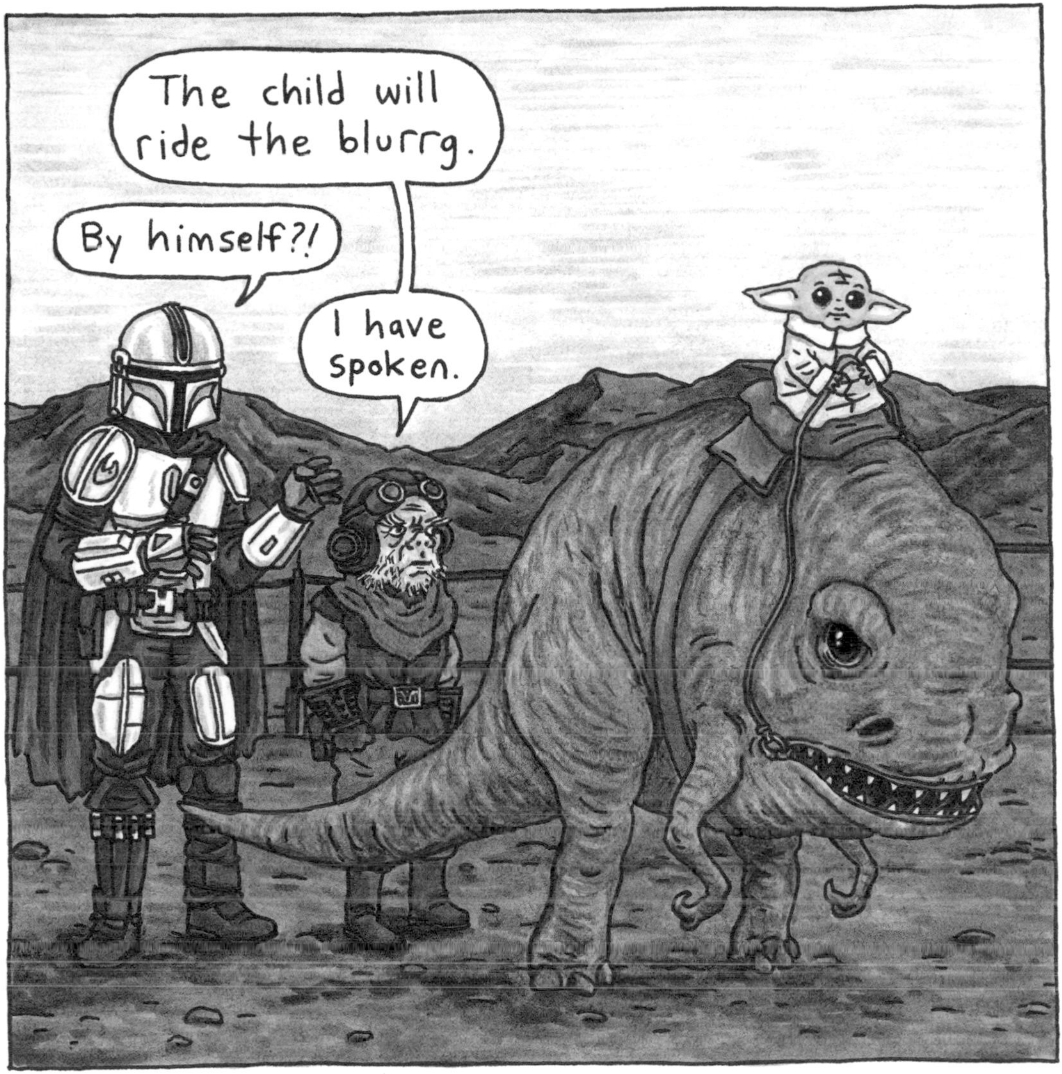
By himself?!
The child will ride the blurrg.
I have spoken.

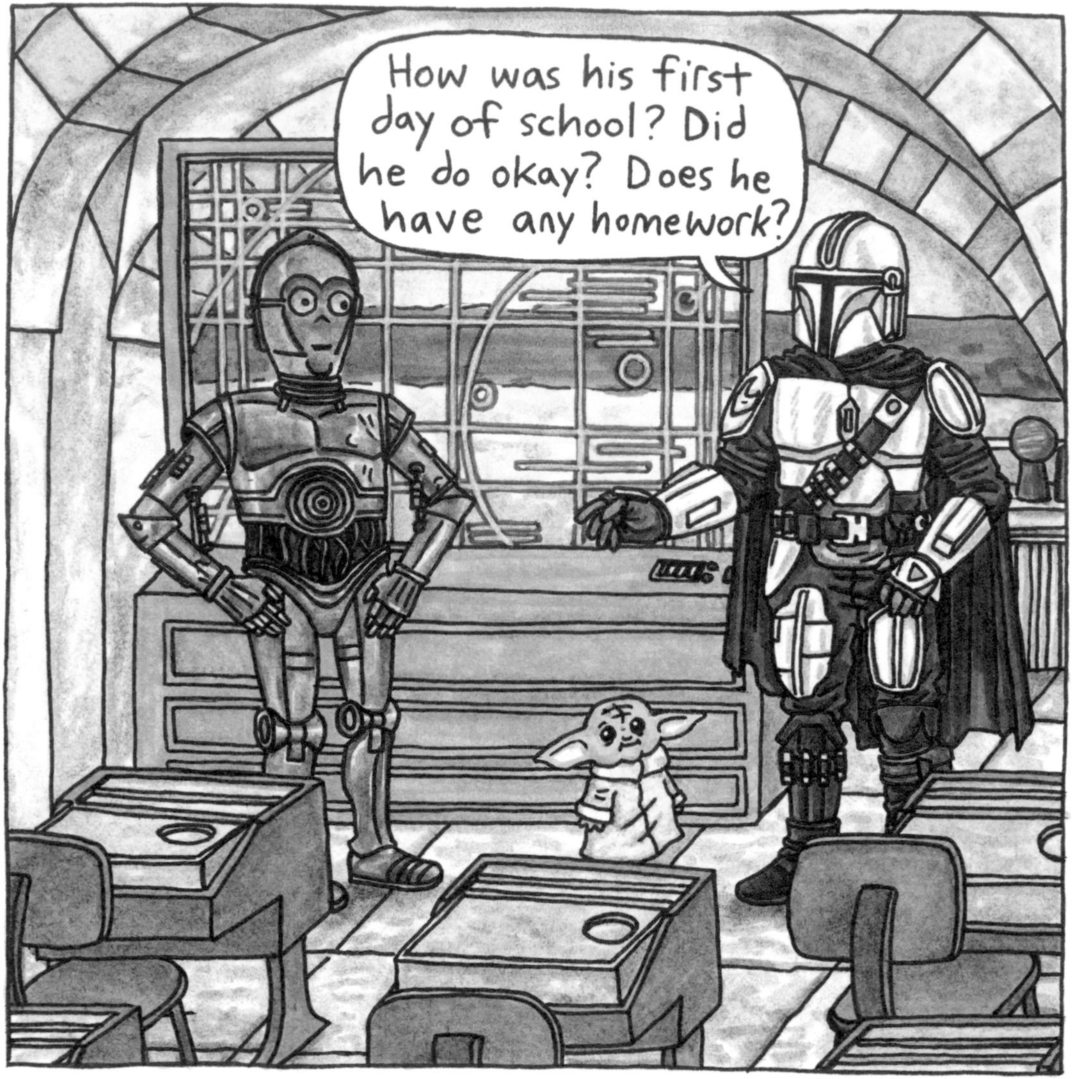
How was his first day of school? Did he do okay? Does he have any homework?

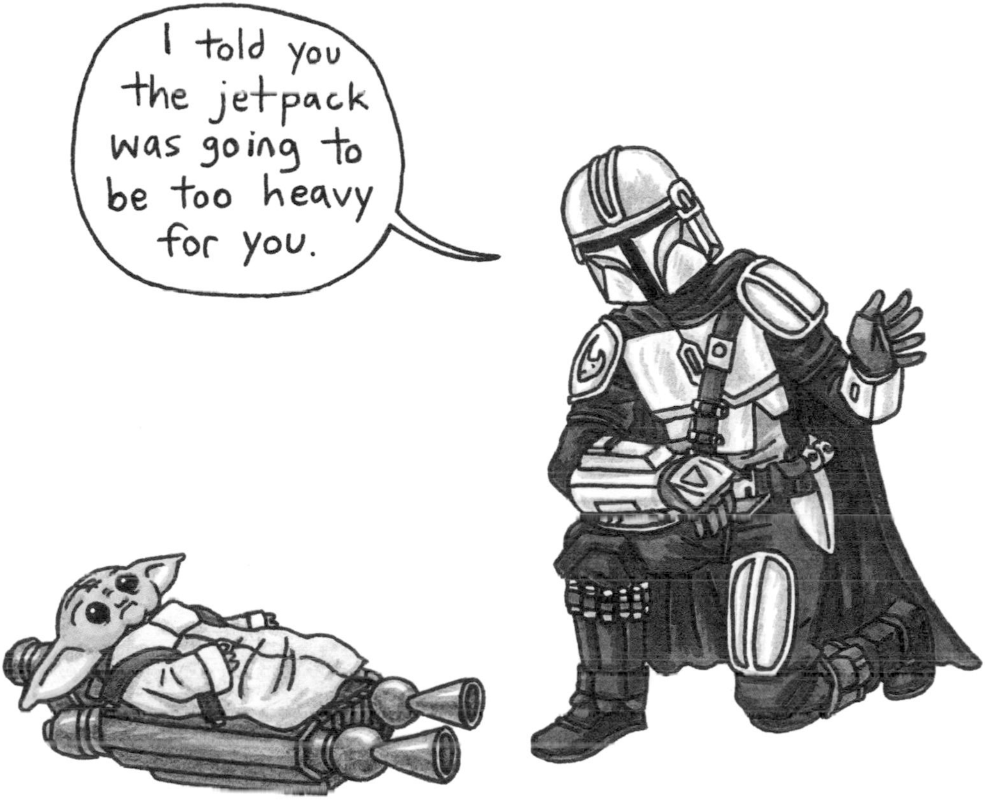
I told you the jetpack was going to be too heavy for you.

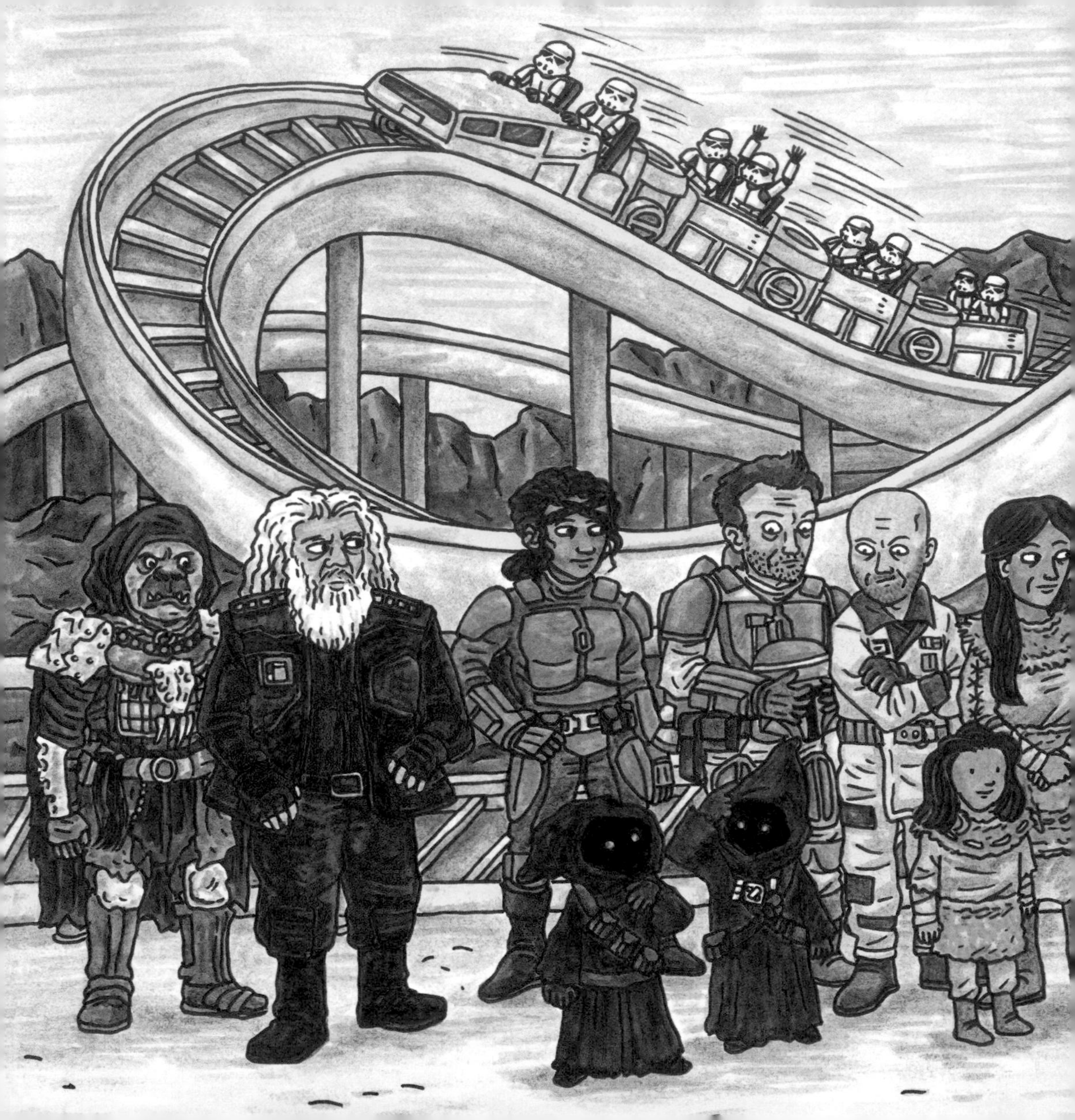

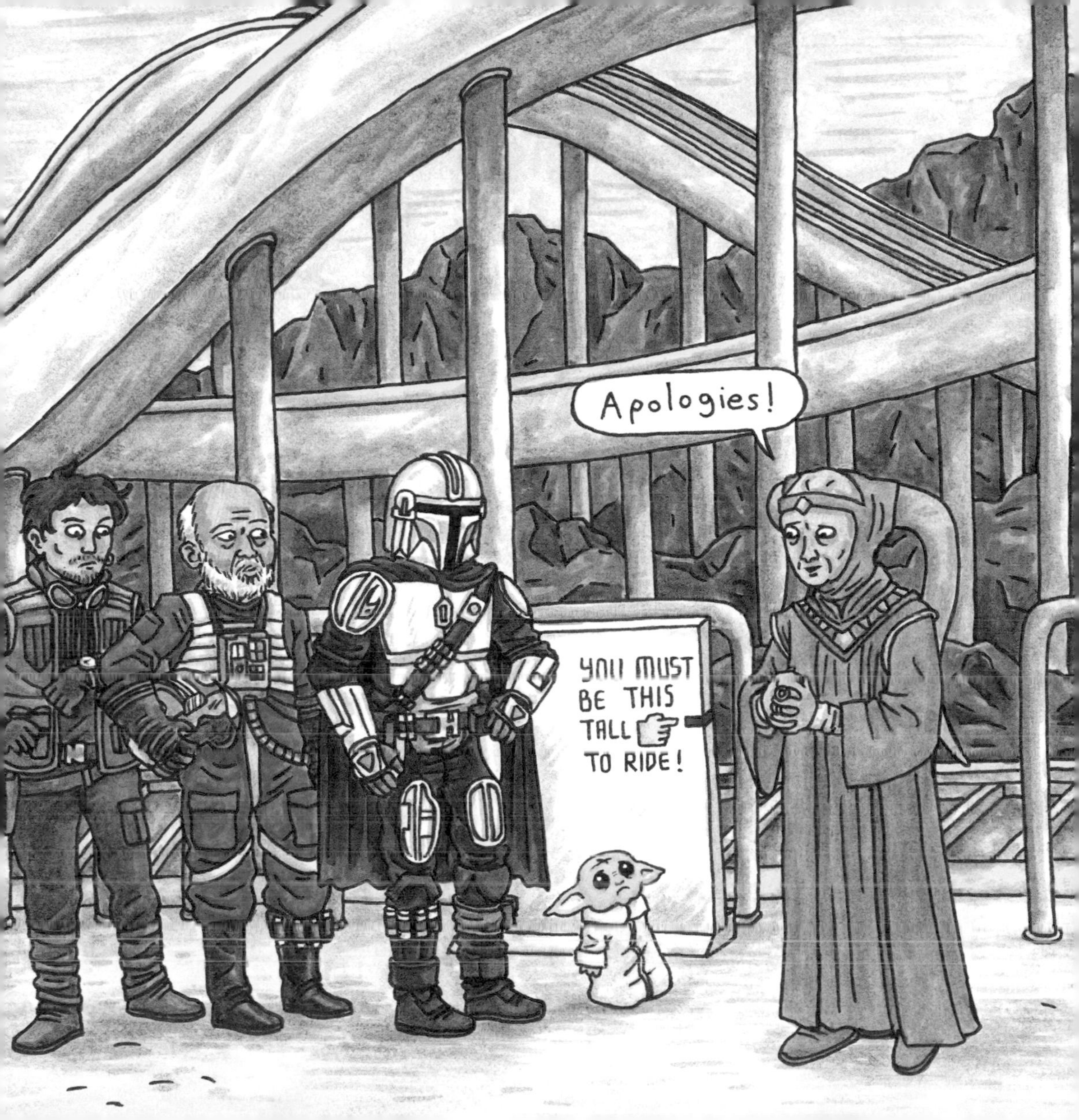
Apologies!
YOU MUST BE THIS TALL TO RIDE!

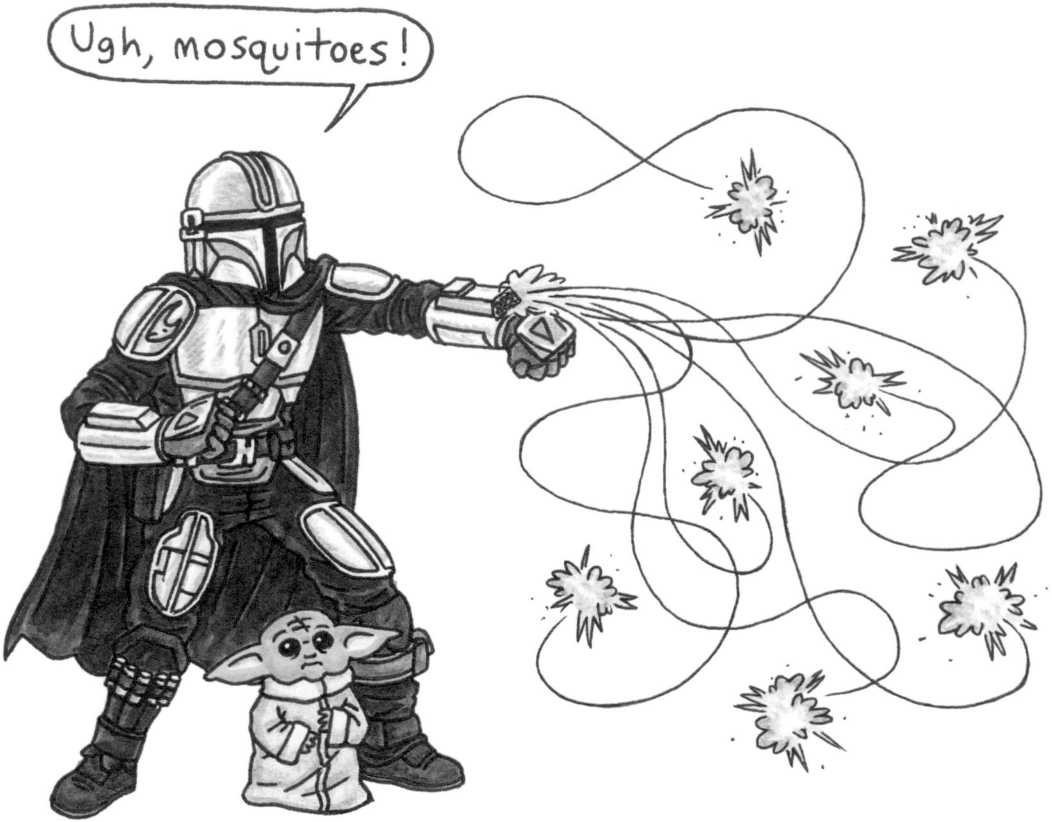
Ugh, mosquitoes!

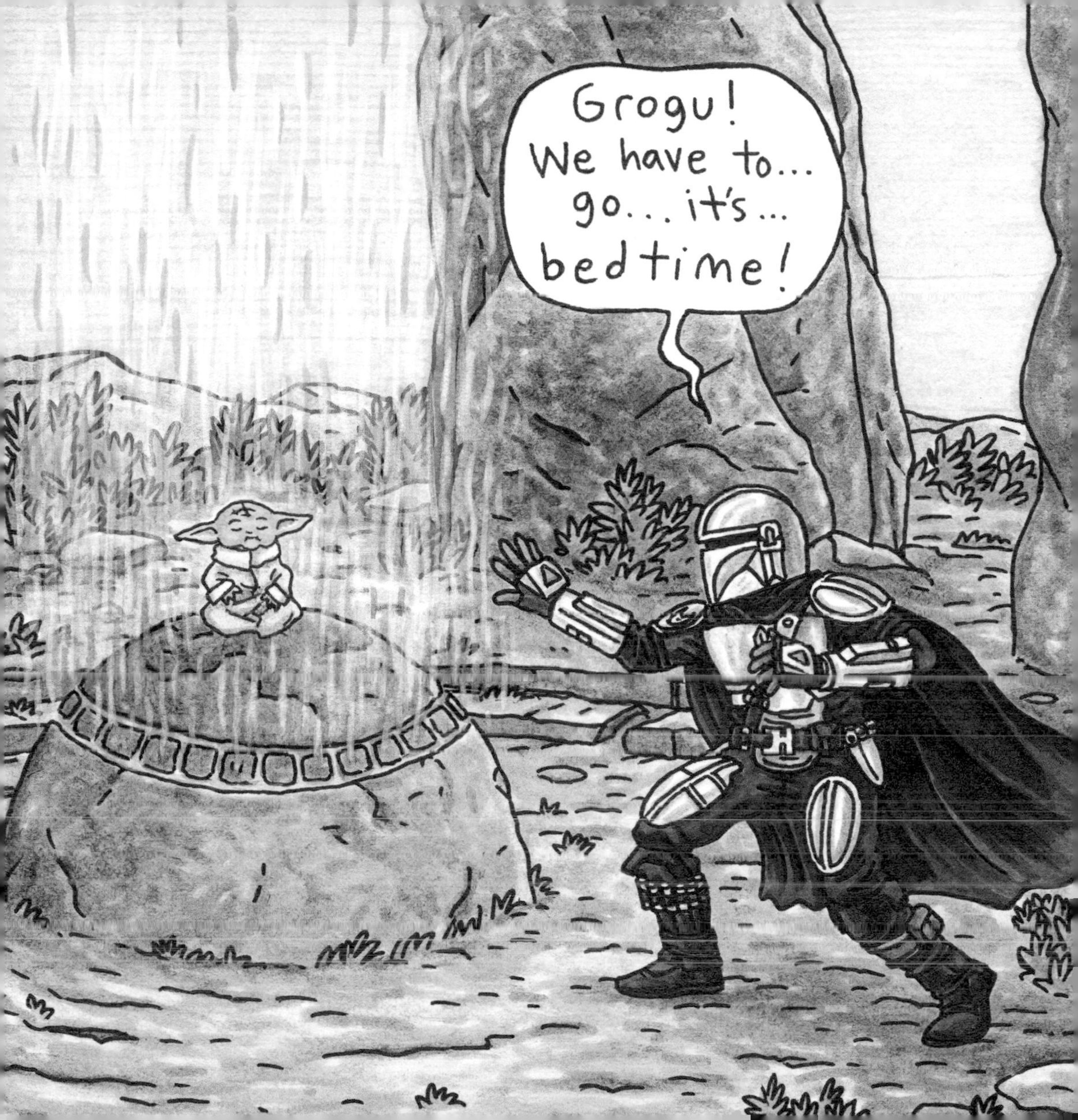
Grogu! We have to... go... it's... bedtime!

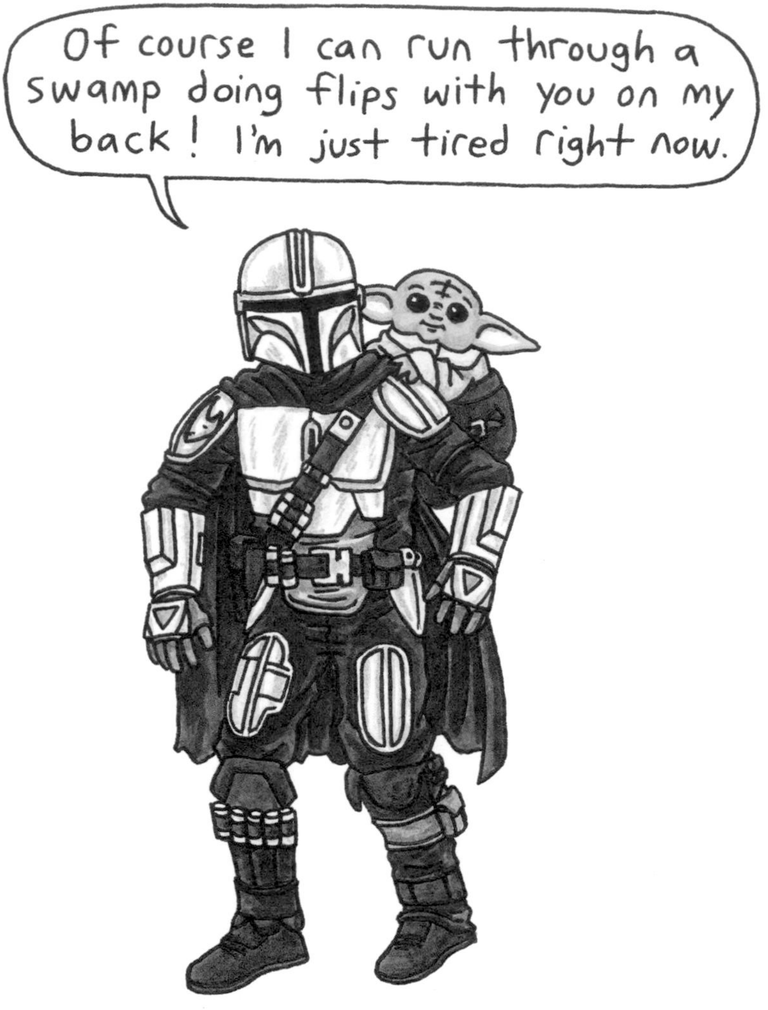
Of course I can run through a swamp doing flips with you on my back! I'm just tired right now.

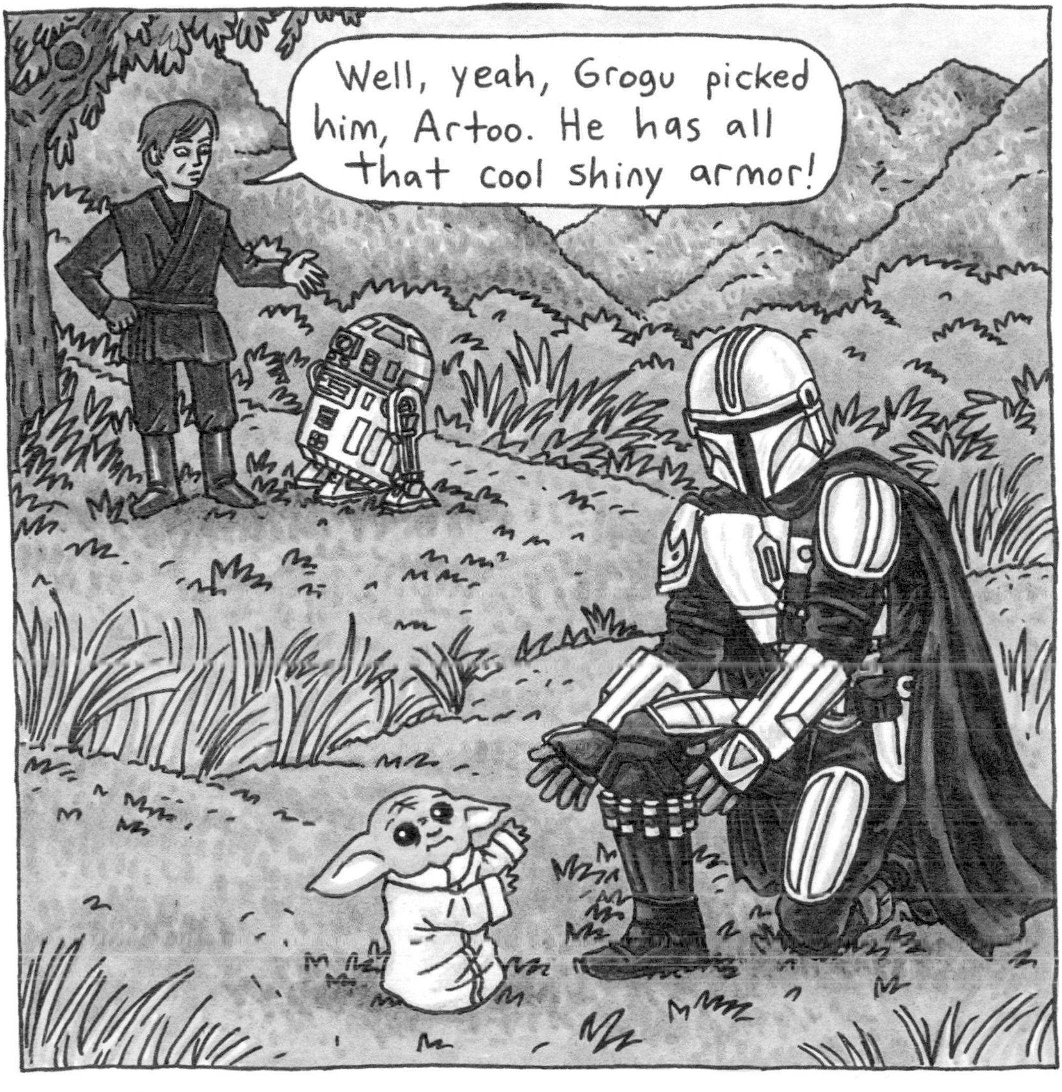
Well, yeah, Grogu picked him, Artoo. He has all that cool shiny armor!

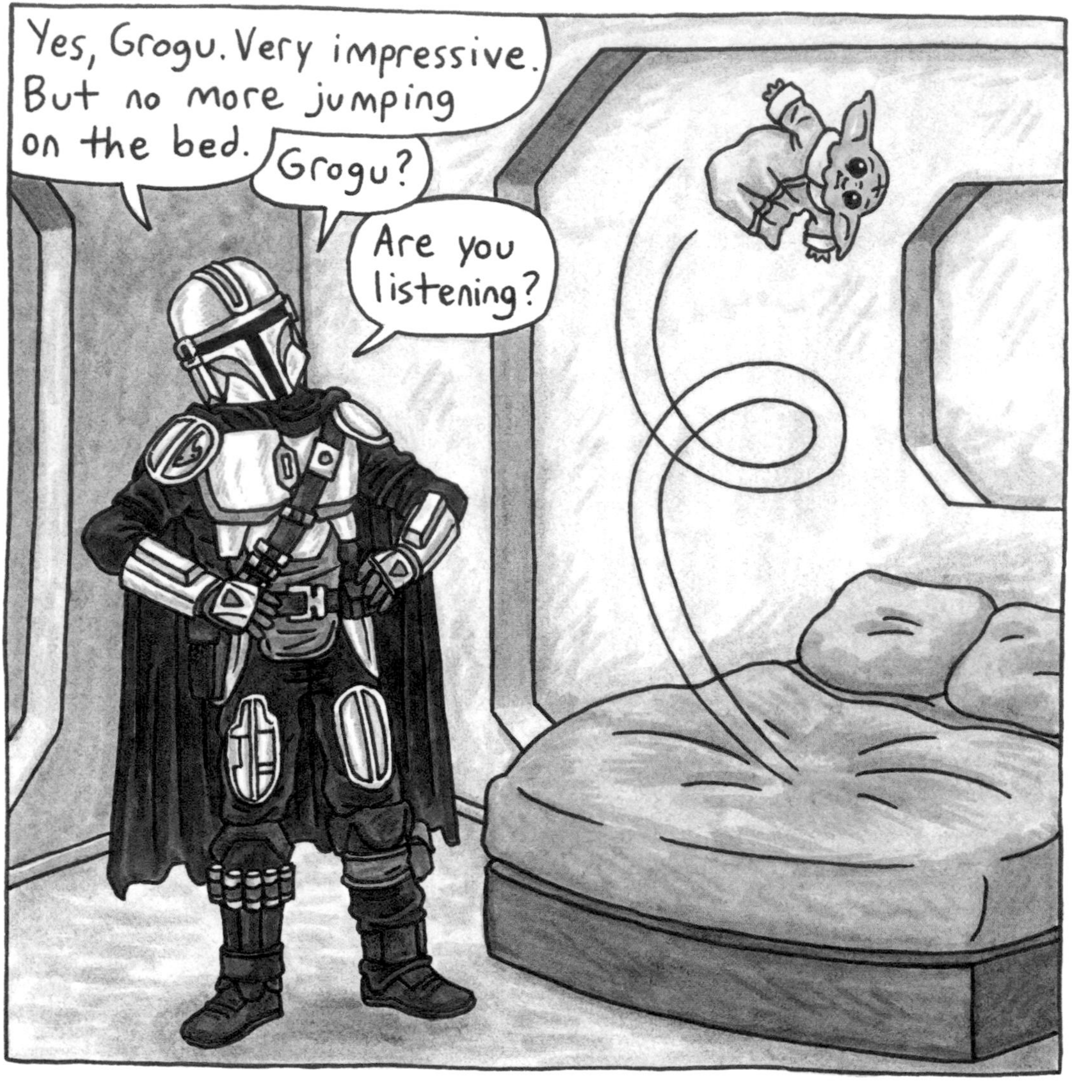
Yes, Grogu. Very impressive. But no more jumping on the bed.
Grogu?
Are you listening?

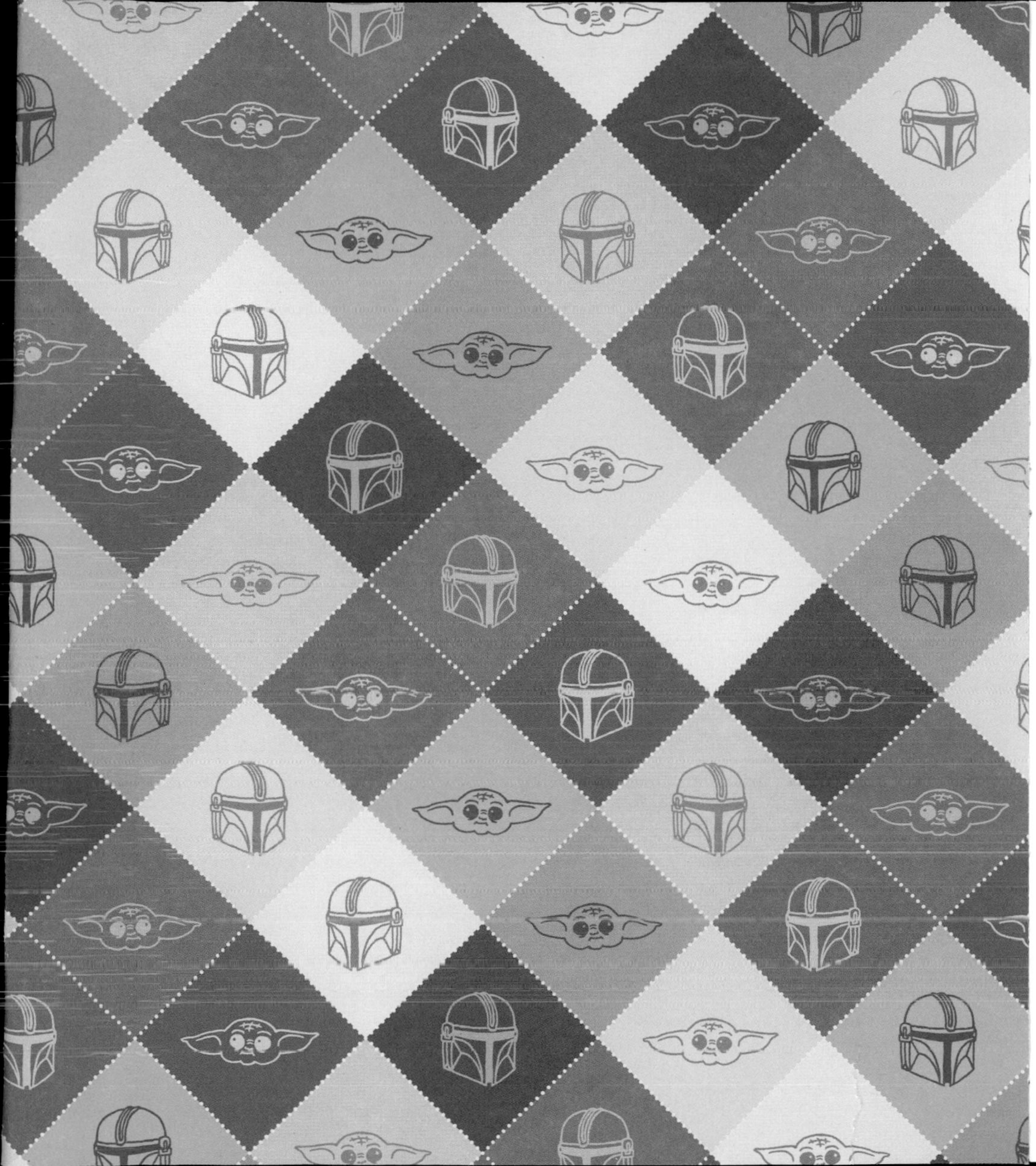

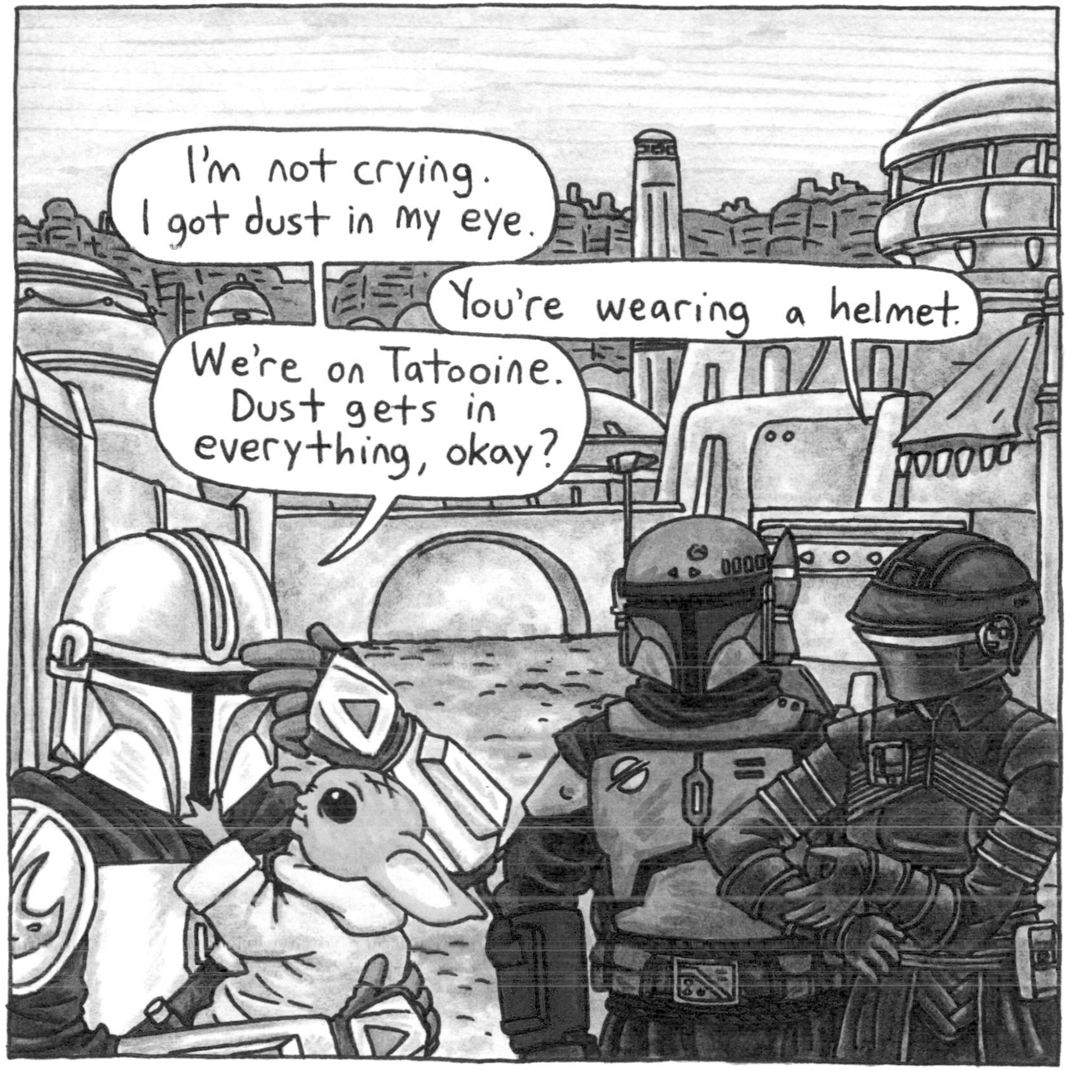
I'm not crying.
I got dust in my eye.
You're wearing a helmet.
We're on Tatooine.
Dust gets in
everything, okay?

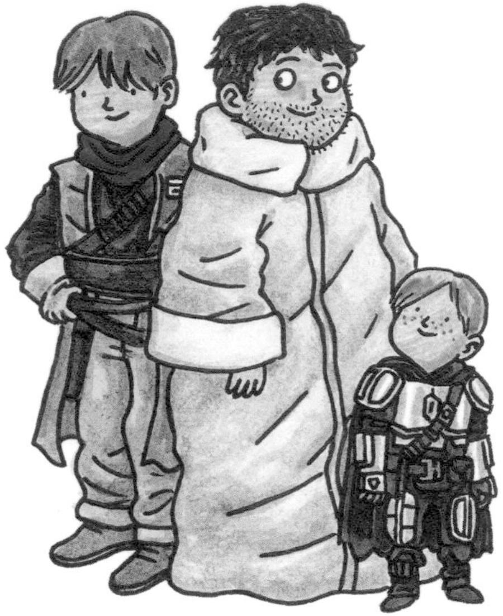

JEFFREY BROWN is the author of numerous autobiographical comics, humorous graphic novels, middle grade series, and several bestselling Star Wars books. He lives in Chicago with his wife and two sons.

P.O. BOX 120
Deerfield, IL 60015-0120
USA

WWW.JEFFREYBROWNCOMICS.COM

ALSO BY JEFFREY BROWN FROM CHRONICLE BOOKS:

Thor and Loki: Midgard Family Mayhem
A Vader Family Sithmas
Rey and Pals
Darth Vader and Friends
Goodnight Darth Vader
Vader's Little Princess
Darth Vader and Son
Cats Are Weird
Cat Getting Out of a Bag

www.chroniclebooks.com

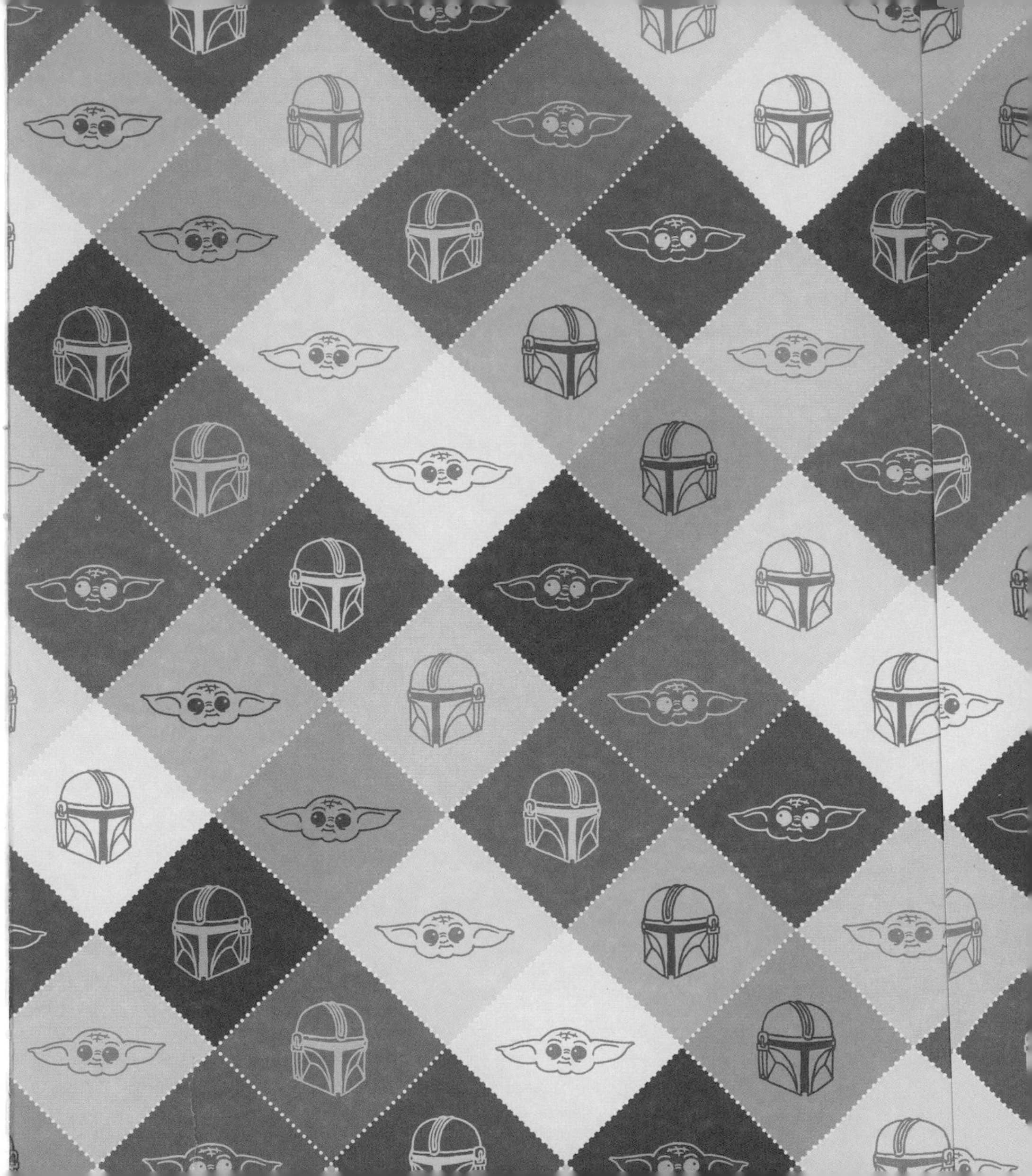

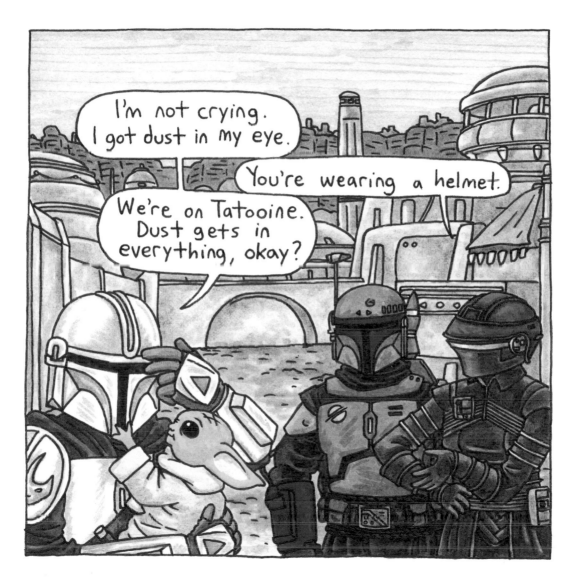

JEFFREY BROWN is the author of numerous autobiographical comics, humorous graphic novels, middle grade series, and several bestselling Star Wars books. He lives in Chicago with his wife and two sons.

P.O. BOX 120
Deerfield, IL 60015-0120
USA

WWW.JEFFREYBROWNCOMICS.COM

ALSO BY JEFFREY BROWN FROM CHRONICLE BOOKS:

Thor and Loki : Midgard Family Mayhem
A Vader Family Sithmas   Vader's Little Princess
Rey and Pals   Darth Vader and Son
Darth Vader and Friends   Cats Are Weird
Goodnight Darth Vader   Cat Getting Out of a Bag

www.chroniclebooks.com

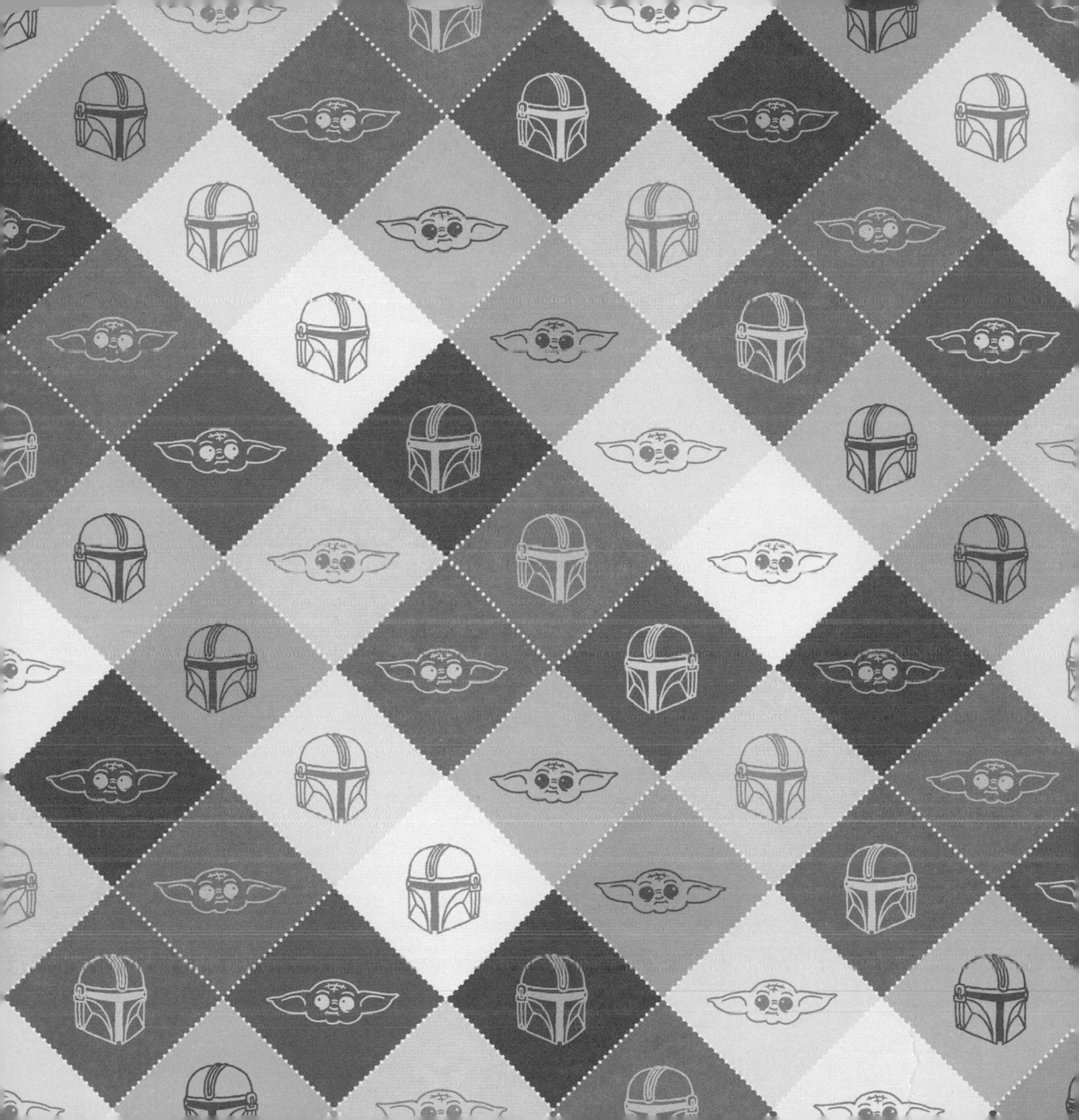

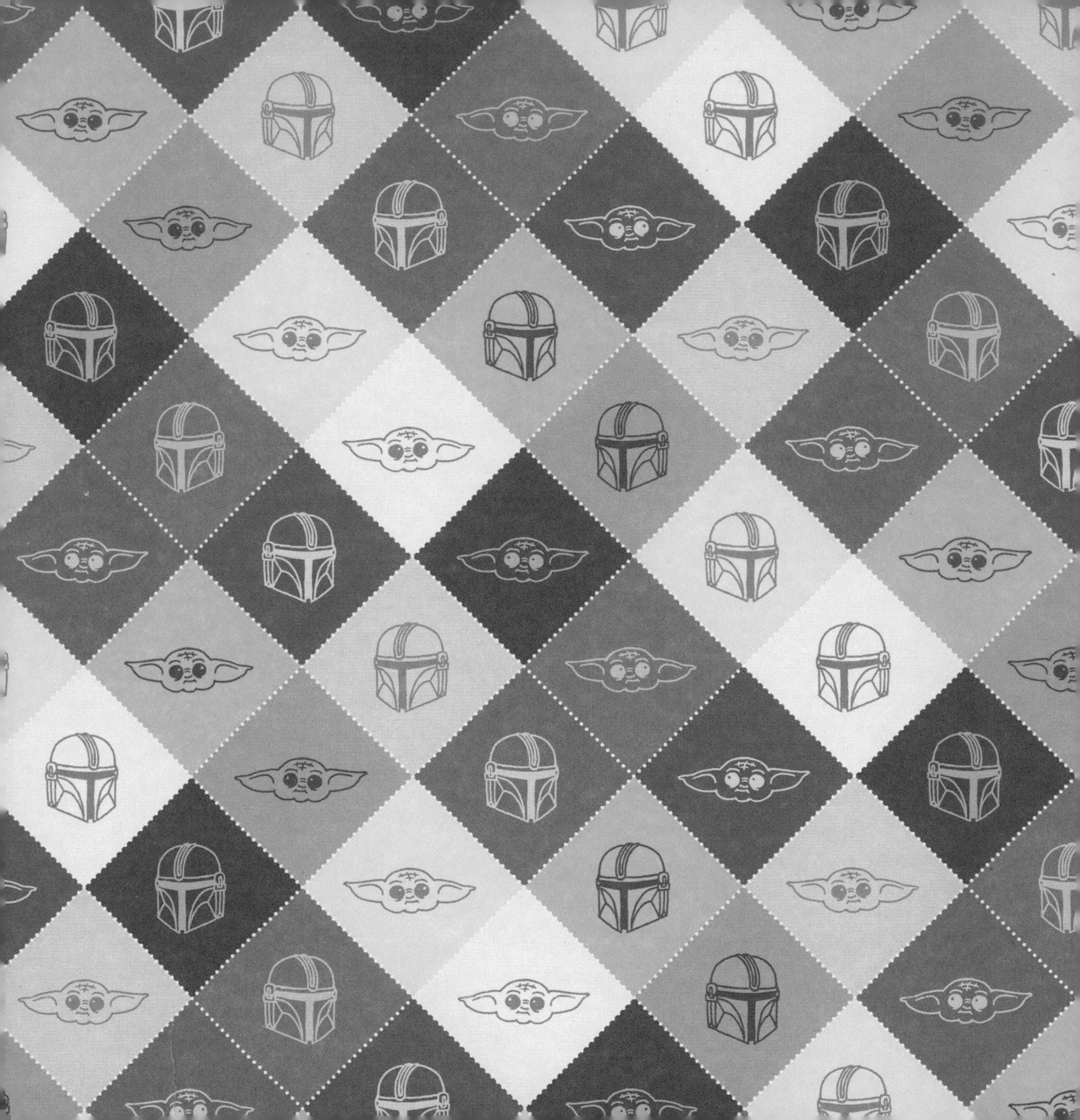